REDISCOVERING ROMANS 9

How Calvinism Distorts the Nature and Character of God

Scott Mitchell

ISBN:9798706493844

Cover design by: Kate Hanley
Editing: Kate Hanley
Printed in the United States of America

"Each will take up a work already begun, and will leave it unfinished. Each is a debtor to those who have gone before, and creditor to those who are to follow. Therefore it behooves us to be filled with humility and restfulness. We must be humble as we remember that no service we render is wholly ours. The conditions which make it possible have been created by others; and indeed in itself is it part of their work. But we must be restful also. None of us can finish anything. The work we do is part of a larger whole, and when our "twelve hours" have run their course, it will not be completed. God will still continue it, and find other instruments. That is the joy of working together with Him."

G. CAMPBELL MORGAN (SEARCHLIGHTS FROM THE WORD)

CONTENTS

FOREWORD

I've known Pastor Scott for almost 30 years. We've been as close as two pastors can be while being separated hundreds of miles by God's calling on our lives. He's been a faithful pastor, committed to his Lord as well as the small portion of the body of Christ at Calvary Chapel of Boston.

There have been many books written on this subject matter so one might ask; "Why one more?" I can think of two reasons. First, we live in a time where most people are easily offended. Add to that a great number of Christians have as their main ethic "just be nice." Given those two conditions, the idea of a good, healthy robust debate and a discussion with arguments, some passion and emotion are avoided or labeled as "not nice." But throughout the Acts and the N.T. epistles we have examples and exhortations to "contend" for the faith.

One of the things that I admire about Pastor Scott is his sincere desire for the truth. We should all follow that example and be on an intense quest for truth. In Rediscovering Romans 9, Scott leads the reader on such a quest and in doing so, not only does he bring great clarity but also gives the reader a model to follow. This book is extremely thorough, full of scripture references and incredibly thought-provoking. As you begin to turn the pages, have a pen ready for notes and be ready to be challenged.

Scott Gallatin

Senior Pastor
Calvary Chapel of the Fingerlakes

BIBLE VERSIONS AND CHAPTER ABBREVIATIONS

Unless otherwise stated, Scripture quotations are from the KJV (King James Version, 1611).

Other Versions:
ESV (English Standard Version, 2001)
HCSB (Holman Christian Standard Bible, NT 1999)
ISV (International Standard Version, NT 1998)
NET (New English Translation, 2005)
NKJV (New King James Version, 1982)
WNT (Weymouth New Testament, 1903)

Longer book titles of the Bible abbreviated as follows:

Genesis – Gen.
Exodus – Ex.
Numbers – Num.
Deuteronomy – Deut.
Chronicles – Chron.
Jeremiah – Jer.
Ezekiel – Ez.
Daniel – Dan.
Zachariah – Zach.
Matthew – Matt.
Romans – Rom.
Corinthians – Cor.
Galatians – Gal.
Ephesians – Eph.
Philippians – Phil.
Colossians – Col.
Thessalonians – Thess.
Timothy – Tim.
Revelation – Rev.

WHY THIS BOOK?

Why did I write this book? Considering there is an abundance of Bible commentaries on the book of Romans, do we really need one more? Good Bible commentaries are always welcome, but my goal in writing this book is not to add one more to the lengthy list. Therefore I address issues beyond the scope of a typical commentary. The focus of this book is more extensive and hopefully more educational. One of my goals is the unveiling of Calvinism so it can be brought into the open. Indeed, when it is understood *what* Calvinism teaches, it is mystifying *why* people believe it. However, when it is properly understood, this only compounds the bewilderment of why it has so many adherents today. Having said that, I hope to clarify the doctrines of Calvinism (ultimately in reference to Romans 9) so unsuspecting saints can escape its subtle grasp before they are lured into its theological trap.

I have many commentaries on the book of Romans, and this actually prompted my concern regarding Romans chapter 9 in particular. I have not discovered a healthy balance of viewpoints regarding God's sovereignty and human responsibility among many Bible commentaries. Therefore, this book challenges the reasons for the lopsided view of Romans 9 toward Calvinistic interpretations. In most cases Calvinistic presuppositions—especially in Romans 9—overwhelm many otherwise sound Bible commentaries. Most are relatively balanced in chapters prior to Romans 9, but once they enter Romans 9, there is an unmistakable shift to Calvinistic interpretive principles. At this point, sound hermeneutics[1] evaporate. I am aware that others have addressed this particular concern; however, many of the commentaries that provide significant value in Romans tend to be a bit scholarly and perhaps inaccessible to many. Therefore, one of my aims is to keep this book within reach, while at the same time explaining some of the more difficult concepts in accessible terms. It is of the utmost importance that Christians rediscover the teaching of Romans 9; this will yield a solid biblical view of God's nature and character. This in turn gives us the Scriptural perspective of God's sovereignty and human responsibility.

It may appear I am concerned with splitting theological hairs, but follow the book all the way through and this will confirm that is not the case. If you stop part of the way through or jump to appealing chapter subjects, it will cause a premature conclusion by avoiding the detailed arguments I develop. I will of course add my own commentary that I believe accurately represents both the nature and character of God through Paul's teaching of Romans 9. This will no doubt put me at variance with many "popular" Calvinistic commentators. However, my interpretation is a direct consequence of following the text and utilizing sound interpretive principles. My intention is not simply to counter Calvinistic views, but to examine Paul's teaching by keeping tight to the text, which provides us the best opportunity to understand Romans 9 as did the Christians who received his letter.

RECOGNIZING THE PROBLEM

Many conservative Calvinistic commentaries do well in their exposition regarding the earlier chapters in Romans, but that shifts abruptly when they enter Romans 9. It is at this point that fundamental hermeneutical disciplines get cast aside to make way for Calvinistic preconditions on the text. The nature and character of God as revealed throughout the Bible ends up changed, as if Paul the apostle somehow had Calvin in mind when he wrote chapter 9. This is a bias that Bible students should be well aware of as they read Bible commentaries, especially by Calvinist leaning authors. In my opinion, the text of Romans 9 does not receive the same hermeneutical care as other chapters in Romans by many Calvinistic commentators. The consequence of this among unsuspecting Bible students leads them to approach the text with the same lack of care resulting in a skewed interpretation. This develops a pattern of ad hoc hermeneutical variation that affects other areas of Bible study as well. Moreover, students tend to follow the methods of esteemed Christian leaders and Bible commentators, but this is one area that students must be well aware. We should exercise the utmost care in approaching the Bible, in particular difficult or controversial passages. Indeed, Romans 9 falls into this category.

In Psalm 138:2 it says, "...for thou hast magnified thy word above all thy name." This is a magnificent statement by God about His own Word. By this Psalm, we conclude that His word reveals Him in the highest glory and reverence. Moreover, it assumes His word is comprehendible. For how else can we give Him glory if we cannot understand His word plainly (1 Cor. 14:9, 16b)? Therefore, *changing* His word when entering Romans 9 will *diminish* His glory. Changing interpretive principles in Romans 9 will put that chapter at variance to other texts in the Bible. Moreover, changing the meaning of God's word will assuredly diminish His name and tarnish His glory. We must therefore handle the Bible with care and reverence. There will be a day when all Christian leaders and Bible commentators will answer to Jesus Christ for what they say, write, and do; this should always be in the forefront of our minds as we interpret the Bible and is a concern I have as well.

REDISCOVERING RESPECT

Disrespect through misrepresentation is nothing new; it happens among people all the time. I cannot count the number of times I have had people misrepresent me, or put words in my mouth that I never said. I have had people tell me what I believe, when in fact I do not. Even when I attempt to correct their claim, many refuse to listen and continue to tell me what I believe. The point here is, if I am disrespected because someone misrepresents me, though frustrating, it is not necessarily going to affect me and I typically do not take it personally. What others claim I believe does not actually change me, it just makes me aware of their opinion. People are always going to have their opinions and I cannot correct everyone's perspective of what they *think* I believe. I have taught enough Bible studies over the past 30 plus years so people can know what I believe and why I believe it. There will always be detractors; as they say, it goes with the territory.

Sometimes disrespectful statements can hurt those beyond the one targeted. If someone makes a disrespectful or inaccurate statement about me and it results in hurt to others, then you have my attention. Affecting others causes the stakes of the case to rise. Moreover, if the claim is against my character and it results in a damaged relationship with someone dear to me (including those God has placed under my care as a pastor) this requires my undivided attention. Not because of how I feel about the personal disrespect, but because of how it affects others who are innocent victims and vulnerable to unnecessary hurt. This issue corresponds to the intention of this book. I believe that Calvinism misrepresents God's character. Though I do not believe Calvinists do this intentionally, the resulting effect is still the same.

When any Christian misrepresents God, it can result in hurt or confusion to believers and effect the presentation of the gospel to unbelievers. Calvinism has a particular problem in this area since their doctrines are notoriously controversial. When a neophyte Calvinist begins to realize the incongruity of the "doctrines of grace" with the clear teachings of Scripture, it can certainly result in confusion. The real problem in this case can be a distrust in the Bible instead of the Calvinistic teachings, since there may not be enough previous Bible education for a fair comparison to take place.

Calvinists typically reject any presentation of the gospel to large groups or crusades because they believe it is deceptive to offer the gospel to those in the crowd who are not the elect. Their actions in rejection of these events spans from refusing involvement to outright picketing as unbelievers enter these events. What does that say to unbelievers? Any concern Calvinists have with the gospel preached to the "non-elect" (in their minds) is a result of their own theological bias and is both unbiblical and illogical. First, in the Bible Jesus and the apostles preach the gospel to groups. We are told that some or many believed, implying naturally that not all believed, or that others rejected. Peter's sermon on the day of Pentecost (Acts 2) is a classic example along with the multiple cities Paul visited on his missionary journeys. His efforts involved crowds of people he preached to, not to mention his visit to Jerusalem (Acts 22). Second, it is illogical to hold the gospel back from anyone through concern they are not one of the elect. Whether it is one or one hundred thousand to whom the gospel is shared, no one knows who will respond positively until after the presentation is made. Moreover, an initial positive response may not be genuine faith; this is only discoverable over time no matter whether it is one or more. There is never a biblical or logical reason to prevent sharing the gospel with anyone when the opportunity presents itself. No one knows or can assume a person will receive or reject the truth.

God has big shoulders and can certainly handle people who do not accurately understand Him because they do not know Him. But, when false or misleading statements made about Him are by those who know Him, this presents a different picture. This can affect the relationship between God and His people, and when this occurs, I think you will have His attention. There is a particular responsibility assigned to pastors, Bible teachers, and Christian leaders to represent Him reverently and biblically. All Christians have the responsibility to engage in "casting down imaginations, and every high thing that exalteth itself against the [accurate] knowledge of God" (2 Cor. 10:5), but those whom God has specifically tasked with overseeing and caring for His flock (1 Peter 5:2-3; Titus 1:9-11) must pay particular attention for the sake of His flock. "The flock of God" (1 Peter 5:2) are His blood-bought people!

False statements and claims about God can easily result in unbelievers rejecting Christ. This however is also a problem in the church among God's people. If there is a place people should be able to go and get a clear understanding of God's self-revelation through His word, it is the church, "the pillar and ground of the truth" (1 Tim. 3:15). His word accurately represents His nature and character; thus, a poor exposition of His word can easily result in misrepresenting Him in the congregation. Paul was well-aware of this problem and spent much of the New Testament (NT) instructing about God and correcting misrepresentations or misunderstandings related to Him. Therefore, this issue requires our utmost attention. Misrepresenting God kept Moses from entering the Promised Land (Num. 20:7-13) after a life of faithful service (Heb. 3:5)—it is a serious matter with God for sure.

REDISCOVERING
THE BIBLE

The church today faces a crisis in respect to their overall low knowledge of the Bible. Unfortunately, I can be a Bible *believing* Christian, but not necessarily, a Bible *respecting* Christian; there is a significant difference and this is the crux of the issue. Our current Christian culture is in dire need of both belief in and respect for the Bible, not just one. There are many teachings among Christians that are truly aberrant and unbiblical, which for the most part they hold to through ignorance of the Bible. Tragically at times, when doctrinal correction is attempted, some still hold to certain extremes no matter how false a teaching is shown to be. We see this phenomenon among the "faith prosperity" promoters. They have successfully wedded their over exaggeration of money, formularistic phrases, and the doctrine of perfect health to the gospel in such a way that they all become synonymous. The core aspects of biblical redemption and all Christ accomplished end up as a servant to financial prosperity, speaking formulas for creating one's own reality, and health guarantees. This is not to say that God does not materially bless or heal His people today—He absolutely does! It is the particular guarantee and overemphasis of money, mantra speech, and health that creates this lopsided, man-centered theology resulting in a severe distortion of the God of the Bible. In this twisted theology, they make God a slave to verbal formulas He ostensibly obligated Himself to fulfill. However, this only works if you believe the promoters and perform or practice all the "special revelation" methods and incantations provided by them. It is a Gnosticism of a different sort with its own esoteric language, concepts, and expectations, which has misguided multitudes. The irony of this theology is that it promotes believing the Bible, though only lip service is given to it. Their sleight of hand presentations masterfully move people away from the Bible and replace it with their own success formulas. They teach people they are faithless or unbelieving if the money, personally desired realities, or health promises fail. The leaders are the ones cashing in on these cunning success formulas; the people just blindly follow. The overwhelming majority of the adherents never receive what the promoters promise. But this is inevitable, since the people are following something the Bible is not teaching. These devotees believe they are respecting the Bible by obeying it as they are "instructed"; however, the doctrines they follow are for the most part, not biblical. They are a blend of what the mind science cults teach[2], along with some mix of Bible stories and selective proof texts (usually the same ones repeatedly). They unveil unique spiritual laws they claim God has mystically "revealed" to them, though they align more with Christian Science than biblical Christianity[3]. These doctrines are presented in a convincing format to lead astray those who seek the extravagant life that is paraded in front of them. Manipulation through slick motivational speech tactics creates promising results with emotionally charged people looking for financial success. The difference in this case is the promoters use God as their lure and develop their success off a misrepresentation of Him. The NT has nothing favorable to say about those who lead God's people astray and make money the main facet of their ministry. Many are wolves in very expensive sheep's clothing. Things do not end well for them.

The god at the core of this peculiar theology is a servant to the prosperity teachers' rules and schemes. They have concocted a fancy potion of legalistic principles (under the guise of grace, faith, and freedom) that craftily overburden the devotees.

Adherents are diligent to "demonstrate faith" and follow the "give-to-get" principle for the promised financial return through stringent obedience to precise formulas. These promoters are experts at communicating their message. They have honed their craft to a precision instrument capable of surgically removing people's finances and smoothly redistributing that money to their own bank accounts. People desiring to have the money and apparent health that these promoters possess follow them like the Pied Piper. Promoters parade the occasional success story before the crowd to demonstrate the "legitimacy" of their teaching formulas like a Vegas winner. The "selling" model is self-promotion (2 Cor. 4:5, 10:12) and anecdotal stories to motivate more "buyers," like a well-oiled Ponzi scheme. People slavishly contribute to "plant a seed faith offering" (is that anywhere in the Bible?), "release the year of jubilee," or "show God your faith" to fill the coffers of these charlatans. The evidence of their success is various multimillion-dollar homes, personal jets and lavish lifestyles, while the vast majority of supporters struggle to make ends meet. It has tragically become a major aspect of the Christian culture today, even though it is revolting. Their misrepresentation of God is so extensive; it is difficult to know where to start correcting it. However, as long as there is an economy to draw on, or desperate people who are willing to believe, it will remain rooted until the tribulation period (Daniel 9:27; Matt. 24; Rev. 6-18) manifests its true colors. The point here is that it is easy to take advantage of vulnerable or naive people. Instead of the gospel of Christ, it is a gospel of money and celebrity that misrepresents both the nature and character of God. There is no other way to convince people to believe this nonsense unless the God of the Bible is made to appear as if He wants His people to believe and follow these teachings, which Paul specifically warns us against (1 Tim. 6:3-10). There will always be false teachings that threaten to derail a Christian's biblical view of God. But when it surfaces as a trend among Christians, and it presents itself in behaviors that disrupts lives and diminishes God's revealed nature and character, addressing it is not an option.

I do not want to be misunderstood here; I am not comparing the Calvinistic interpretation of Romans 9 with the "faith prosperity" gospel. But I am comparing the effect of disruption among Christians when God is not represented biblically. To know God as He wants to be revealed can only be through a systematic and contextual study of His word. Any teaching that does not properly allow the Bible to say what it wants will inevitably result in a distortion of who God is. However, our particular focus in this book is the Calvinistic distortion of Romans 9. The "faith prosperity" teachers will have to wait.

THE IMPACT

One might ask, "what's the big deal; does it really matter how I view Romans 9? It's only one chapter. Is it really going to change my understanding of the whole Bible?" The answer is, yes, it certainly may and with many Christians already has! From Augustine to Calvin to current theologians, there have been varying views on Romans. It would be a mistake to think that the crucial teaching of Romans 9 is just an isolated chapter with little effect on the rest of the Bible. The biblical history drawn on in the chapter and the conclusion Paul draws ties together the major thread of redemption and Israel's reception of it. Moreover, Paul directly addresses the nature and character of God in his typical use of an interlocutor's questions. Therefore, this book is not just another commentary on Romans 9. This book is really an appeal to allow the Bible to reveal God in all His glory, sovereignty, and magnificence, as He—borne along by the Holy Spirit (2 Peter 1:21)—wants to be known through the agency of chosen Scripture writers. One's viewpoint of Romans 9 becomes more of a barometer to their view of the whole Bible and God's nature in particular. Therefore, it is our responsibility as Bible students to labor, paying attention to all the details God has put in His Word for us to discover. Uncovering these gems of truth will have great reward in both understanding and the resulting heart felt, awe-inspiring worship of our Creator and Savior. How can we in good conscience do less? Additionally, tied to our grasp of the truth will be our application of it in daily life. What we believe finds expression in what we say and what we do —it is unavoidable.

This brings us to the crux of the issue. Whenever Romans 9

is taught publicly or read privately, Calvinistic presuppositions are almost a given. The baggage of their interpretations has grown deep roots in Christian resources over the years. One fruit of this tree seems to be an apprehension among Bible commentators and theologians to counteract too much of the Calvinistic position at the risk of being branded as a Pelagian, semi-Pelagian, or some other form of works-oriented heretic. The fear is unwarranted; we should never apologize for solid biblical exposition. My exposition on Romans 9, I expect, will draw criticism. It's assumed both sides will have opinions, as everyone always does, yet both are necessary to analyze for a complete understanding. Books and statements are there for evaluation and should be able to stand up to proper scrutiny.

One of the unavoidable issues in reference to Romans 9 is how views contrary to Calvinism end up mischaracterized; this unfortunately has been a typical criticism. Some Calvinists wrongly express opposing positions consistently. They provide an overly simplistic explanation of opposing views, many times belittling them as if anyone holding a contrary position is because of a lack of scholarship. However, this is the quintessential strawman so regularly presented by some popular Calvinists against opponents. When opposing non-Calvinists, some Calvinists assume the only other position must be a form of Pelagianism—what else is there? In their view, either God is meticulously determining all things or man is somehow in control and confusing works with grace. Therefore, for some Calvinists, they view a person who claims to be a Christian, yet rejects Calvinism, as a person who in some aspect must be working for their salvation or at a minimum, doctrinally immature. In their mind, if a person exercises "their own faith" in response to the gospel, and does not believe they are exercising the particular faith that God "gives them," it is viewed by many Calvinists as a work. Why? Because it does not fit into the "the doctrines of grace" framework that Calvinists have constructed.

Views opposed to Calvinism tend to be mocked as if they are not within the realm of biblical possibility. The Calvinist usually comes to the rescue against opposing views and provides what in their mind is the proper biblical explanation. But are they really providing a proper *biblical* explanation? Biblical explanations are supposed to clarify, illuminate, and produce understanding, which should yield practical biblical application. Many times Calvinistic explanations are more confusing and illogical than the alternative. Moreover, they keep going back to Calvin and fitting the Bible into his highly skewed brand of deterministic theology. At this point however, they are not providing an *explanation* of the Bible; they are making a *declaration* of Calvin's views. Often repeating slogans by Calvinist teachers—while at the same time belittling opponents—resulting in nothing more than pontifications that entertain and lull the Calvinist faithful into thinking only they have the truth, while the truth actually continues to elude them.

Calvinists often use circular reasoning with their deterministic perspectives in Romans 9, as well as other areas of the Bible. Their arguments tend to become repetitious, wearisome, and dull. I have listened to Calvinists debate the merits of Calvinism against opposing views, and their reasoning is circular. They argue that opposing views cannot be true because they counteract Calvinistic determinism[4] – which is not evidence against opposing views. Then they assume that Calvinism is true since it is deterministic and argue from that context. In formal logic, this is called "begging the question" because it assumes as true what someone is trying to prove without evidence or reasoning in a circle. Calvinists have presuppositions that are so entrenched that at times it is difficult to have a meaningful dialogue. This is because they use the same words as a non-Calvinist, such as *grace, works, sovereign, foreknowledge, election, predestination,* and *faith,* but fill them with different meanings that are esoteric Calvinistic definitions. The exclusive definitions of these words used by most Calvinists cause confusion with many non-Calvinists. I am not convinced that all the Calvinists that use the esoteric meanings of terms are using them deceptively; I believe that some of them just accept the definitions without any thought to the Calvinistic preloading. However, from the knowledgeable Calvinist's perspective, I think it is time that the theological smoke and mirrors be put aside and they just say what they mean because they know better. However, this is a tough pill for most of them to swallow because the doctrines of Calvinism are not palatable for most Christians once they truly understand what Calvin actually believed and taught.

My lack of adherence to Calvinism will no doubt label me by some as unable to "tolerate the truth." However, the truth is I cannot accept the unbiblical ideas promoted by Calvinists when they grossly mishandle parts of the Bible and foist them upon the unsuspecting or inadequately equipped saints. As mentioned above, many times this results in both the misguidance and hurt of sincere but naive Christians. They latch on to Calvinism because a Calvinist friend persuades their naïveté; unfortunately, many of these "teachers" are not equipped themselves to teach the unsuspecting student. They attempt to convince their friend that if they *truly* want to understand what mature Christian doctrine is and grow in grace; they need to adhere to what Calvin taught. They claim Calvinism is where the meat of the truth of Christianity lies. This is a sad case of the theologically blind leading the naively blind in many cases. Additionally, since many Calvinists will tend to convert Christians to Calvinism instead of unbelievers to Christ as an evangelistic practice, vulnerable Christians should know exactly what they are being lured into. Indeed, the truth is much simpler and straightforward than Calvinism teaches. There is no need to obscure it in special Calvinistic terms or heavily preloaded theological determinism. The truth in the Bible is simple and straightforward; therefore our theology should correlate to that.

PERSONAL EXPERIENCE

My first years as a Christian I went back and forth between Calvinism and Arminianism or some combination in-between. As I read Calvinistic authors I greatly respected, I wanted to be a Calvinist. As I read non-Calvinist authors I greatly respected, I moved away from Calvinism. As a relatively young Christian, I realized I needed to make a decision based on how I understood what the Bible teaches and not what other people believed. So I accumulated the books from both sides, and worked my way through them. I discovered there were certain perspectives from a Calvinistic aspect that just did not align with the Bible in its plain and obvious sense. Because of the years it took to work my way through these issues, I now try to help inquiring Christians of the important theological features and save them some time and possible frustration. Today I am neither Calvinist nor Arminian theologically (though I find myself having more in common with the Arminian perspective because of its position on libertarian free will). I prefer to follow the Bible in its obvious and plain teachings and not through the framework of one person's theological views, be that Calvin, Arminius or anyone else. That kind of practice I believe is inherently flawed and spiritually dangerous. Christians should understand the basics of varying theologies so they have a comparison for concluding the truth of Scripture with the least bias possible. This is not a short study, but a lifelong learning of the depths of God's Word, which is truly inexhaustible.

At this point in my life, I have had many conversations

with Christians who are confused as to what Calvinism *actually* teaches. When I take a few minutes to explain what the doctrines are, many are shocked that a Christian would even believe them. When I explain the Calvinistic system, I tell them what Calvin himself teaches, and how the T.U.L.I.P. acronym expresses the points of Calvinism for clarification. However, providing the multiple perspectives and various nuances within Calvinism today is *not* my goal; there are just too many. Having said that, I do not believe I mischaracterize the essential Calvinistic positions in this book. While there are a multitude of theological nuances within the Calvinistic framework of the Reformed tradition, addressing each one is beyond the scope of this book. Thus, I will address the more traditional views within Calvinism in my critique. Calvinists disagree among themselves; therefore, what Calvin taught and most Calvinists adhere to today is what I address.

I think we need to remember we are not bound to Calvinism and its rooted concepts in order to be orthodox--quite the contrary. In reference to Romans 9, there are other more accurate non-Calvinistic ways of understanding it, and in turn the rest of the Bible! Comparatively, this is not the public school environment where they only allow one view (evolution) in science class and any alternate view—such as Intelligent Design —as a nonviable pseudo-science *a priori* (i.e. without evidence). Evolution is not science based on supportable lines of evidence, but a blind commitment to materialism without investigation or challenge. Intelligent Design could easily unseat the blind commitment to materialism that frontloads the Darwinian belief system, but it is never allowed the opportunity in public schools. Therefore, we need to be careful. This is the church of Jesus Christ and there should be the freedom to discuss viewpoints on these important biblical doctrines, as long as they do not conflict with the essential doctrines of the Christian faith. The exchange of doctrinal positions should be without the belittling of those who in any way oppose Calvinism, as if an opposite view is unthinkable or ridiculous. On the contrary, it is not only "thinkable" to oppose the extremes of Calvinism, but in this writer's opinion, it is the only "thinkable" response-- hence this book. People have the freedom to follow Calvinistic teachings, but I think they need to be aware that there are other biblical options. However, many times Calvinists squash the opposition before there is any opportunity. In this case, removing choices aligns with their theology.

I have read, heard, and watched the exchange between theologians on various topics such as Dispensational vs Covenant theology and Reformed Calvinism vs Arminian or non-Calvinistic Evangelicalism. When done as mature Christians the outcome is educational and can add to our faith, no matter what side is favored. When done with arrogance and a predisposition to treating the opposite perspective as stupid and moronic, there is nothing of value in the discourse. This kind of exchange results in the polarization of listeners and fracturing of brethren that is unnecessary and a violation of the very teaching of Scripture (Prov. 6:19). I can—and have—disagreed with other Christians on particular doctrinal issues, and for those who know me well, I have strong opinions. However, I would never break fellowship or refuse to welcome a believer that had different opinions within the pale of orthodoxy. I know people (some at our own church) who believe differently than I do on particular doctrinal positions, but frankly, it's not an issue--for me anyway.

As it relates to Calvinism, I have had Calvinistic brothers over the years in secular jobs and church fellowships. We never discussed any of the theological differences because no one was pushing the issues from either side. We just served the Lord and any theological variance we held to did not create a varied operational difference. The same holds true for my Arminian friends, as I am not in full agreement with all their perspectives either. It is only when people make their theological positions the main features of Christianity that it affects fellowship.

When Calvinism or Arminianism *becomes* Christianity for people, it is almost impossible to have fellowship in Christ; their agenda persistently overwhelms the conversation and diverts the relationship. It is no different with eschatological systems, when that is the driving agenda all the time, conversations can make you feel like you are in the tribulation, though I am personally pre-trib. All who study to refine their doctrinal understanding in theology and eschatology will have varying nuances in their views—what else is new? These variances are necessary so that education and adherence to the truth can result (1 Cor. 11:19). But why make them a test of fellowship if they are not a test of orthodoxy? The only time to break fellowship, aside from heresy, is if the holder of a particular view (even one that is orthodox) motivates people to be divisive. When that occurs the destructive result is division that disrupts the Body of Christ. In that situation, we have clear instructions from Paul the apostle how to respond (Rom. 16:17).

I realize that Calvinism has become popular among many young people, and much of their justification for the reliability of their doctrine is because of the quantity of followers trailing after popular Calvinists. I am reminded of a statement James Sire made, "The fact that a teacher has followers points first to popularity, not reliability".[5] Though Sire was speaking in the context of belief systems that are beyond Christianity, the truth of the statement is applicable within Christianity as well. Quantity is not quality, and attendance is never a test for accuracy. History is a great teacher; it reminds us that majority vote is never a test for truth. In the Nicene Council (AD 325), the majority of followers were initially sided with Arius the heretic, who taught that the Son of God was *not* equal to God the Father. The smallest group out of the three represented (a third group was in-between and followed Eusebius, the church historian) were those following Athanasius of Alexandria, who taught that the Son of God was equal to God the Father. Today, Christian orthodoxy is belief in the equal essence of both God the Father and God the Son (and God the Holy Spirit, i.e. the Trinity). But in the 4th century, that was not the majority belief until it was hammered out in the Nicene Council, expressed in the Nicene Creed. Thank God for faithful men who were willing to stand up for the clear teaching of Scripture and not bow to the popularity of a belief based simply on numbers alone.

REDISCOVERING CALVINISM

This might seem like an odd topic choice for a book that is arguing against Calvinistic teaching. However, defining Calvinism is critical to understanding the perspectives from which they derive their theology. There is a lot written about the history of the development of certain Calvinistic perspectives, but the simplest way to understand what Calvinism teaches is still the acronym T.U.L.I.P. This acronym describes the 5 Points of Calvinism in response to the points advanced in 1610 by the "Remonstrants," a movement that split from the Dutch Reformed Church in the early 17th century. These Remonstrants were followers of Dutch theologian Jacob Arminius, who had departed from the Calvinistic interpretations of the Bible. When the Remonstrants put forth their "Points" (originally 7, easily reducible to 5 for comparison), the response of the Calvinists were their own 5 Points. The table below explains the contrast between the basic points of those who followed Jacob Arminius and the response of the Dutch Reformed Church with the classic 5 Points of Calvinism. Here is a brief explanation with each to help clarify.

POINT	REMONSTRANTS (ARMINIAN VIEW)	REFORMED (CALVINIST VIEW)
1	TOTAL DEPRAVITY (man cannot save himself apart from the grace of God)	TOTAL DEPRAVITY (man has no ability to respond to God in any way)
2	CONDITIONAL ELECTION (man is chosen based	UNCONDITIONAL ELECTION

	upon God knowing he will exercise faith in Christ)	(man must be chosen from eternity because he has no ability to choose Christ)
3	UNLIMITED ATONEMENT (Jesus' atonement is for all and renders everyone savable)	LIMITED ATONEMENT (Jesus' atonement is only for those God chose from eternity)
4	PREVENIENT GRACE (God works by grace to move the sinners' free will to faith in Christ, but is resistible by man)	IRRESISTIBLE GRACE (man cannot resist God's grace once it is upon him, and he will choose Christ by faith)
5	CONDITIONAL PERSEVERANCE OF THE SAINTS (faith is the condition of salvation; therefore, if faith is abandoned, so is salvation)	PERSEVERANCE OF THE SAINTS (the elected saints will persevere until the end, their works demonstrate their election and security)

What is important to notice regarding the Calvinistic perspective is how they define Total Depravity, better understood as the Total *Inability* of the sinner to respond to God. This includes the inability to respond to the conviction of the Holy Spirit, the gospel of Christ, or the witness of believers. Calvinists see the unregenerate sinner comparable to a dead person in a coffin who is unable to respond to anything at all. Therefore, it only makes sense to them that the sinner has to be previously chosen (elected) and subsequently made alive so that "after" they are spiritually alive, they can then exercise faith in Christ--but not before. This understanding of how a person is regenerated is opposite that of the clear teaching of Scripture. The Bible never has regeneration prior to faith; it always follows faith, which is the condition of receiving salvation. The response of faith required is the basis of Paul's theology in Rom. 4:3, which is spoken of Abraham in Gen. 15:6, and foundational to all Paul's teaching on justification by faith. In Eph. 2:8, note that in the following grammatical explanation faith is *not* the "gift"

REDISCOVERING ROMANS 9

given by God. In Gal. 6:15, the new creation is after explaining in the epistle that faith is required for justification. In 1 Peter 1:23, people are born again by the word of God, and faith comes by hearing the word of God (Rom 10:17). In John 3, with the explanation of the new birth by Jesus, v. 3 states, "unless you are born again, you can't see the kingdom of God"! Nichodemus' response in v. 9 is "how can these things be?" Jesus provides the answer. v. 15, 16, and 18: "whosoever believes." In other words, by faith.

The normal presentation is to believe in order *to* have life. Saving faith in Christ always and immediately results in regeneration, and any and all lost sinners can believe in Christ and be born again (Jn. 1:10-13, 16:8, 12:32, 20:30-31; Eph. 1:13). John's comments to his audience: "But these are written, that ye might believe that Jesus is the Christ, the Son of God; and that believing ye might have life through his name" (John 20:31), and Paul's exhortation to Timothy: "Howbeit for this cause I obtained mercy, that in me first Jesus Christ might shew forth all longsuffering, for a pattern to them which should hereafter believe on him to life everlasting" (1 Tim. 1:16) are good examples. Therefore, saving faith in Christ is *before* and results in regeneration (i.e. being born again, Eph. 1:13). God draws sinners to Jesus Christ by his Holy Spirit to afford them opportunity to make the choice by faith. This is by the conviction that the Holy Spirit brings (John 16:8), the preaching of the gospel (Rom. 10:13-17), and the grace that provides enough illumination so all can understand what is being presented by God by way of truth and the gospel (John 1:3-5,9). Note that faith comes by "hearing the word of God." In this particular context, the gospel is the topic! Faith does not come by the regeneration of the Holy Spirit first, but in response to the gospel. The whole context of Romans 10 cries out that "whosoever" hears can believe and be saved, but they cannot believe unless they hear the gospel (Rom. 10:14). Indeed, upon hearing they can also reject the gospel as Isaiah says (Rom.

23

10:16).

There is plenty of evidence prophetically (OT and NT), philosophically, and scientifically through creation (Psalm 19, Rom. 1:15-16) of God's existence. The "image of God" was not entirely destroyed in Adam's fall (Gen. 9:6), thus man's innate reasoning ability coupled with the enabling work of God through the Holy Spirit is sufficient for man to believe. On this point, Blaise Pascal said:

> God has willed to redeem mankind and to open salvation to those who seek him. But men render themselves so unworthy of it, that it is just that God should refuse to some because of their hardness of heart what he grants to others out of a mercy not their due. Had it been his will to overcome the stubbornness of the most hardened, he could have rendered them unable to doubt the truth of his essence, in revealing himself manifestly to them…

> It had not then been just that he should appear in a manner plainly divine and wholly capable of convincing all men, but neither had it been just that he should come in so hidden a manner as not to be recognized of those who sincerely sought him. He has willed to reveal himself wholly to these, and thus willing to appear openly to those who seek him with their whole heart, and to hide himself from those who fly him with all their heart, he has so tempered the knowledge of himself as to give signs of himself visible to those who seek him, and obscure to those who seek him not.

> There is enough light for those who wish earnestly to see, and enough obscurity for those of a contrary mind.

> The prophecies, the very miracles and proofs of our Religion, are not of such a nature that we can say they are absolutely convincing. But they are also of such a kind, that none can say that it is unreasonable to believe in them. Thus there is both evidence and obscurity to enlighten

some and blind others.[6]

The verse Calvinists stand on as a proof text that a person must have spiritual life "before" they believe is Eph. 2:8,9 which states, "For by grace are ye saved through faith; and that not of yourselves: it is the gift of God: Not of works, lest any man should boast." Calvinists understand that the "faith" Paul mentions in verse 8 is the "gift" that is given, which then enables belief. They support this interpretation by quoting Eph. 2:1: "And you hath he quickened, who were dead in trespasses and sins." They understand this to be the sequence of how God saves, instead of reading properly that it is God who saves. Beginning at verse 1 they interpret the series of verses through verse 8 as the sequence of how salvation takes place instead of stating the fact of what must take place for salvation to occur. If you notice in most Bibles, there are *italicized* words in verse one, which means they are added by translators for clarity, but do not appear in the text itself. So verse one literally reads, "And you who were dead in trespasses and sins." The words "He made alive" are taken from verse five and added into verse one for *clarity*, not *accuracy*. Therefore, Paul is not detailing the sequence of how the salvation process proceeded, but the facts of why salvation is necessary. When read without bias, verses 1-7 inform us that we were spiritually dead, separated from God by nature, we lived in a world separated from God, but because of His tremendous love and mercy He made us alive in Christ, united us to Him, and in the ages to come we will learn more about His great mercy. God's greatest act of mercy is expressed in this verse. Even though we were spiritually dead, God made us alive in Christ. Note that this occurred by grace, which connects the act with faith, shown in the phrase "by grace you have been saved." ""Grace" explains how God operates. It refers to "undeserved favor" and is a constant reminder that God does not manifest acts of mercy toward people because they deserve them."[7] Verse eight explains how this happened by grace. However, this mention of grace is anticipated from verse five with the phrase in parenthesis "by grace you have been saved." Thus, knowing the facts Paul presented, there is a simple solution to correct this erroneous view of Calvinists.

Calling upon the classic grammarians to solve this dilemma for us will clearly provide the necessary information we need to understand verse eight properly. In Eph. 2:8, the gift "refers not to [faith] pistis (feminine) or to [grace] charis (feminine also), but to the act of being saved by grace conditioned on faith on our part" (Robertson's Word Pictures).[8] The gift is "not *faith*, but the *salvation*" (Vincent's Word Studies).[9] The gift is "not your faith," but "*the gift*, viz. of your salvation...*it is a gift, and that gift is God's*" (Henry Alford Greek NT).[10] "The salvation is not an achievement but a *gift*, and a gift from none other than God" (Expositors Greek NT by Nicholl).[11] The word "gift" [DORON Strong's #1435] under heading number 1 (d), "of salvation by grace as the gift of God, Eph. 2:8" (The Expanded Vine's Expository Dictionary of NT Words).[12] These classic grammarians define the *gift* in Eph. 2:8 as salvation, which is in direct conflict with so many modern Calvinists as they claim it refers to faith. Additionally, two more quotes are very significant in this regard. The first is a fuller quote from Kenneth Wuest, the former Greek teacher at Moody Bible Institute. He says regarding Eph. 2:8:

> The words, "through faith" speak of the instrument or means whereby the sinner avails himself of this salvation which God offers him in pure grace... The word "that" is touto, "this," a demonstrative pronoun in the neuter gender. The Greek word "faith" is feminine in gender and therefore touto could not refer to "faith." It refers to the general idea of salvation in the immediate context. The translation reads, "and this not out from you as a source, of God (it is) the gift." That is, salvation is a gift of God. It does not find its source in man. Furthermore, this salvation is not "out of a source of works." This explains salvation by grace. It is not produced by man nor earned by him. It

is a gift from God with no strings tied to it. Paul presents the same truth in Romans 4:4, 5 when speaking of the righteousness which God imputed to Abraham, where he says: "Now, to the one who works, his wages are not looked upon as a favor but as that which is justly or legally due. But to the one who does not work but believes on the One who justifies the impious, his faith is computed for righteousness. (Wuest's Word Studies Vol. 2)[13]

Finally, our analysis would not be complete without hearing from John Calvin himself. In His commentary on Eph. 2:8, he says:

And here we must advert to a very common error in the interpretation of this passage. Many persons restrict the word gift to faith alone. But Paul is only repeating in other words the former sentiment. His meaning is, not that faith is the gift of God, but that salvation is given to us by God, or, that we obtain it by the gift of God.[14] (Calvin's Commentary on Ephesians 2)

It is unfortunate that the modern Calvinists do not adhere closer to their founder they so revere on such a linchpin issue of their doctrine. Indeed, it would save a lot of misdirection and misunderstanding regarding fundamental Bible exposition in the critical subject of salvation.

In response to the T.U.L.I.P. acronym of Calvinism, the clear statements of the Bible should easily clear up any confusion. The lens through which Calvinists read the Bible results in altering what the Bible says to accommodate the preloaded baggage of their system. Walking through the 5 Points should easily reveal the contrast of the variant views of their theology compared to the clear teachings of Scripture.

RESPONSE TO
TOTAL DEPRAVITY

Death means separation. Physical death is the separation of the conscious life from the physical body and spiritual death is the separation of the person's consciousness from God. Because it is through the *spirit* of man that he relates to God, and not through his body, this separation in the Bible is *spiritual* death. God is not physical so man cannot "reach out and touch him" (John 1:18, 4:24). Having said that, spiritual death is not equal to physical death in the operational sense. In other words, a spiritually dead person can still function and relate, even to God in some aspects, but a physically dead person has no body capability at all. Those spiritually dead in the Bible are able to respond to God. Our sin causes this separation from God as Isaiah says, "your iniquities have separated between you and your God" (Isaiah 59:2). Norman Geisler makes the point that, "Adam and Eve, for example, died spiritually the moment they ate the forbidden fruit (Gen. 3:6; cf. Rom. 5:12), yet they were still alive and could hear God's voice speaking to them (Gen. 3:10). So, whereas the image of God in fallen man is effaced, it is not erased. It is marred, but not destroyed. Thus, unsaved persons can hear, understand the Gospel, and believe it to be regenerated or made alive in a spiritual sense (Eph. 2:8–9; Titus 3:5–7)."[15] David Guzik notes that:

> We err if we think that dead in trespasses and sins says everything about man's lost condition. It is an err because the Bible uses many different pictures to describe the state of the unsaved man, saying he is:

- Blind (2 Cor. 4:3-4)
- A slave to sin (Rom. 6:17)
- A lover of darkness (John 3:19-20)
- Sick (Mark 2:17)
- Lost (Luke 15)
- An alien, a stranger, a foreigner (Eph. 2:12, 2:19)
- A child of wrath (Eph. 2:3)
- Under the power of darkness (Col. 1:13)

Therefore, in some ways the unregenerate man is dead; in other ways he is not. Therefore, it is valid to appeal to all men to believe.[16]

The separation caused by spiritual death necessitates that God remedies the problem because man cannot. Man cannot save himself or atone for his sin. A sinner has nothing to offer from their own depraved nature to provide God by way of atonement to remove any of their sin. Moreover, removing sin does not automatically infuse spiritual life; this is a separate aspect of redemption. This is why Jesus Christ needed to complete the work of man's redemption if there was to be any redemption for man at all. On the cross, His work enabled the possibility that man could receive by faith the work accomplished on his behalf. Yet it is man's own faith as all the texts of Scripture describe, not a faith that is given to him so he will then believe. The analogy Calvinists make of equating physically dead people to spiritually dead people is mixing metaphors. They conflate two different types of death (separation) theologically into one. However, this spiritual separation is not the particular total depravity Calvinists claim it is.

Calvinists define *depravity* based on their conflation of the two deaths, concluding that spiritual death is equally unable to respond to prompting, no different from the body in the casket. Upon this false foundation, they have built their theological presupposition. It follows naturally that Calvinists would understand a man could not respond to the gospel if death is as they define it. But as we will examine, the Bible tells a different story. Additionally, we must maintain accurate theological definitions so we can properly correlate our terminology. Thus, *depravity* in Calvinism correlates better to our understanding of *ability*. Therefore, total depravity is better understood as total inability. In this way, a more accurate explanation of the topic under discussion is comprehended. So though some Calvinists may not like the change in words from depravity to inability, by their own operational description, it is exactly what they mean. Some simple examples from Scripture should make the case against this idea. Remember, to disprove total inability, not all Bible verses have to deny it completely. There only needs to be some selection that clearly denies it. The burden is on Calvinists to make the case for total inability. Thus, it is not required that non-Calvinists show that every verse in the Bible refutes the position. If there are Scriptures that clearly reveal God interacts with man, and it is without question the man's own faith is exercised, Calvinism fails its presuppositions. This being the case and the thrust of this book, it is concluded that there is an ability in man to exercise his or her own faith that Calvinists deny exists. When a person is accused of murder, it does not need to be proved that they murdered multiple people or a certain amount before they are found guilty of murder. The prosecution just has to prove that one murder was committed by the accused for guilt to be established. On the opposite side of the case, if the defense attorney can establish reasonable doubt that their client had committed a murder, then guilt cannot properly be established. It only takes one murder proved or reasonable doubt established for the case to go in either direction. This is why James says, "For whosoever shall keep the whole law, and yet offend in one point, he is guilty of all" (James 2:10). James makes the point that one violation of the law makes one guilty of all the law. Not that they had to break *all* the laws to be guilty, but that they are a lawbreaker because they broke at least *one*. Though it is much different in the severity of the crime, the person that gets the parking ticket is a lawbreaker equal to the murderer. Obviously, we have a system established so the punishment will equal the crime, but both equally broke the law and thus are lawbreakers. The weight of the crime does not detract from the category they place themselves in as lawbreakers. The only difference is in the assigned punishment based on the level of the crime, but both are equally guilty of breaking the law. Therefore, as we examine some passages from the Bible, if God requires the faith of individuals in any capacity, they do not possess a total inability to respond. In these following passages, it is clear that God does not respond for them. Nor does He make them respond in a Calvinistic fashion. As we read the text in a normal way, without any Calvinistic assumptions, these people are exercising their *own* faith. Examples like this destroy the esoteric definitions used by Calvinists claiming total depravity is the inability to respond to God with a person's own faith.

Jesus healed two blind men in Matt. 9:29. It says, "Then touched he their eyes, saying, According to your faith be it unto you. And their eyes were opened." Jesus did the healing with His own power and capability; however, the blind men had no way to be healed without Jesus doing the miraculous work. He required them to have their own faith to receive that healing; otherwise, His statement to them makes no sense. It was "according to your faith," He said. There is only one way to understand this. You can attempt to manipulate it or try fancy word gymnastics, but in the end, it is still their own faith that was required for the healing to take place. His words become deceptive and meaningless if He told them healing was due to their reception of it by faith, but then supplied the faith to them—it certainly cannot be both. What He did not say was "according to your faith that I am giving you," etc. Thus, if we compare the process of salvation to the blind men, we see a correlation. God offers salvation through the gospel and when man receives it by faith, God justifies the sinner (Rom. 5:1). Trying to make this a determinative interchange between God and the sinner makes a mockery of God's offer and distorts His word.

How about Matt. 17:20? Here we have the situation of the disciple's inability (this is actual inability) to help the man with the demon-possessed son. The father of the boy approached the disciples for help after Jesus descended from the mount of transfiguration. They could not cast out the demon; thus Jesus came to the rescue and ultimately delivered the boy. After Jesus cast out the demon, His disciples came to Him and asked why they were unable to do it. In response, "Jesus said unto them, Because of your unbelief: for verily I say unto you, If ye have faith as a grain of mustard seed, ye shall say unto this mountain, Remove hence to yonder place; and it shall remove; and nothing shall be impossible unto you." A chastising statement like this is absurd if God is the one holding back faith from the disciples to accomplish the task. Their inability was due to the lack of exercise regarding their own faith. Do we realize that imposing a determinative view of theology puts Jesus at odds with God as well as the disciples? If God determines who will and will not have faith, Jesus should not have corrected the disciples, for it would only have been God's will for them to fail. But this is surely not what the text says.

So there is no misunderstanding here, in reference to belief itself, a person can believe anything he or she wants, but that will not necessarily have any effect in their life. In other words, people believe lies all the time and people live out their lives believing myths. In reference to believing the gospel, more accompanies this transaction. For example, if I believed in Jesus for eternal life, but there was no gospel and the Holy Spirit was not involved with that belief, nothing would result from it. The gospel must be an actual truth previously established based on God's work of redemption, and His involvement is required in the transaction of belief for it to have the result of regenerating spiritual life. Eternal life is not a matter of just believing something, it is a matter of believing the specific gospel of the true Jesus Christ and the impartation of spiritual life by the Holy Spirit when that belief occurs. Regarding the gospel, the NT is clear: unless the Holy Spirit convicts of sin and the need for Christ, no regeneration will take place. The Holy Spirit is fully involved with the individual in the transaction of faith, and once the individual exercises their own faith, the Holy Spirit imparts life to them--regenerates them. Man on his own will never come to the place of realizing what Jesus has done for him without the combination of the conviction of the Holy Spirit (John 16:8) in the power of the truth of the gospel message (Rom. 1:16). In a similar way, the blind men could have believed whatever they wanted about healing, but no healing would have occurred, unless Jesus healed them. It would have only been wishful thinking on their part; thus Jesus was the One that did the healing, not their faith. Their faith was required to receive it. His healing of their blindness was in response to their faith, but that was only because He initiated the offer in the first place. Similarly, the sinner could not receive spiritual life unless the Holy Spirit regenerated him or her, for He is the Regenerator, not their faith. God requires man to exercise faith in the message of the gospel to be born again. Therefore, in both the healing and salvation examples, God transacts the benefit in response to the belief of the individual, based on the offer. It is not a determinative work of God contextually or grammatically in either situation.

Applying Calvinistic determinism to many of Jesus' statements makes them incomprehensible and frankly, silly. If we decide we cannot take Jesus at His word, we are on dangerous ground and have no biblical justification for it. When atheistic evolutionary scientists tell us we need to remember that what appears to be design in biological systems is not actually design, we take that as an absurd and illogical claim. Richard Dawkins stated, "Biology is the study of complicated things that give the appearance of having been designed for a purpose."[17] Francis Crick, the co-discoverer of DNA, said: "Biologists must constantly keep in mind that what they see was not designed, but rather evolved."[18] But these statements are absurd and contrary to both logic and evidential investigation which science lives by. Why would I cast aside my senses, previous knowledge, experience, and reasoning from what I know to be true, and subject them to the bias of an atheist who rejects design because it contradicts his Darwinian presuppositions? Moreover, they are asking me to use my senses, previous knowledge, experience, and reasoning to believe their statements, but nothing else. This is tantamount to madness. Yet somehow, I am supposed to do the same thing when I read the Bible because Augustine and Calvin developed a philosophically determinative system of interpreting Scripture that apparently has more authority than the very Bible they interpret. This thinking is illogical, self-contradictory, and of equal madness, and should not be considered for a moment. These Calvinistic presuppositions when applied to many texts of Scripture make it impossible to comprehend what the Bible clearly says. How silly it would be if I were required to run every Bible verse through the "Calvin-meter" to make sure I apply Calvin's determinative framework before we can actually know what divine inspiration has said. This would result in a mischaracterization of God and confusion among all Bible students.

How did the early church fathers know how to comprehend the Scriptures before Augustine and Calvin? They certainly did not have the deterministic framework prior to those men. In fact, the only people that believed in this type of philosophical determinism were the Gnostics – which does not speak well of this theology. I suggest we run Calvin's interpretation through the "Bible-meter" and see how he survives that instead of making the Scriptures subject to one man's interpretation.

The question is, can a man exercise faith that is "his own" without God exercising it for him or making him believe? To answer "no" creates multiple theological problems as demonstrated. First, the regenerating work in man that

Calvinists claim must happen prior to a person exercising faith (which God actually does for them under Irresistible Grace), would render people in the Old Testament (OT) unable to have faith, since they are not regenerated in the NT sense. Nevertheless, God reached out to them and required faith from them (Isaiah 65:2). We cannot overlook the fact that Abraham is the basis of Paul's theology for justification by faith. Second, it would cause us to interpret the statements of Jesus and Paul in a way that is entirely nonsensical. Jesus and Paul blame unbelief on people who refuse to believe, and even chastise them for their hardheartedness. Nevertheless, Calvinists deny this even with the presentation of solid biblical evidence (Matt. 11:20-24; John 8:46, 9:41; Acts 28:23-28; Rom. 1:19-20). Third, every charge of unbelief that frustrates the will of God (ex. Heb. 3:10) would be nothing more than God frustrating His own efforts since He did not "elect" those people who persist in unbelief. Moreover, every warning in the Bible would be nothing more than powerless words devoid of meaning since the warning is from God to those who will not believe. Yet according to Calvinism, he has previously decided to not allow them to believe.

Calvinists have to come to grips with the fact that they cannot reconcile their theology with the normal reading of many texts. For example, in 2 Cor. 1:10, Paul, speaking of the great danger he and his ministry team fell into, said: "He [God] has rescued us from a terrible death, and he will continue to rescue us" (ISV). Why would God need to rescue Paul? If God determined Paul to be in the circumstance of "terrible death," why did he say God rescued him out of it? Did God put him in it so He could then rescue him out of it? A more natural reading of the text would be that "the prince of the power of the air, the spirit that now worketh in the children of disobedience" (Eph. 2:2) caused Paul's situation through those "children of disobedience" the devil works through to accomplish his ungodly deeds. That being the case, it makes more sense that God is the *Rescuer* from and not the *cause* of Paul's dread. Indeed, we would think it is strange if a firefighter locked someone in a burning house only to then turn around and rescue the victim from a life-threatening blaze. Moreover, it would be deceptive and wicked, not to mention criminal, to plot such evil. Are we to charge God with that kind of plotting? If determinism is true regarding the method of God's sovereign control of every meticulous detail of people's lives, God is the one who put Paul there in the first place, only to then remove him out. Not a very flattering picture painted of God.

In another example from 1 Thess. 2:18, Paul informed the Thessalonians that his multiple attempts to visit them failed because Satan hindered him. He said to them, "we would have come unto you, even I Paul, once and again; but Satan hindered us." How is this possible under the Calvinistic system? How can Satan hinder anything contrary to God's sovereign purpose? Moreover, if Paul says it was Satan, what is God's involvement in this? If the claim is Paul had an intent that was not God's will for him, this does not solve the problem; it only confuses the issue further. For in that case, God's determinative sovereignty in Paul's life was ineffective. Additionally, Paul was assigning a determinative work of God to the devil. According to Calvinist's own explanation of this issue on free will from the Monergism website,[19] God not only determines Paul's actions, but also those of Satan. However, determinative actions stem from the will of those acting; this is how Calvinists explain God's work in the regeneration process (i.e. Irresistible Grace). They claim God makes people spiritually alive by regenerating them, which in turn, changes their will to want to believe. So if it is claimed that God overrides the wills of both Paul and Satan to impose His own will to be done in every situation, this again solves nothing for Calvinists. It puts God in the position of causing Satan to hinder Paul, while at the same time making Paul attempt to visit Corinth multiple times. This now challenges the sovereignty of God according to the Calvinistic perspective. Is God not powerful enough to affect people by changing their nature to move their will (Irresistible Grace), just change their will directly, or in some way determinatively cause all these events? Calvinists cannot have it both ways. They cannot alter the determinative method by which God works in one person and alter the method in another when it does not fit the application of their theology. But this is the crux of the issue when attempting to make the Bible applicable through the Calvinistic lens. From a deterministic perspective, God fixes the crises He creates. Interpreting these examples through the Calvinistic lens forces us to imagine a God in cross-purposes with Himself—hardly the God revealed in Scripture. Perhaps without realizing it, Calvinists have created a God that is constantly working against His own purposes. Yet at the same time, they claim no one can alter His will or purpose. So, which is it? Both are not logically, or scripturally, possible! A theology such as this results in a god that is at a minimum, confused, conflicted and manipulative. This does not honor God, nor does it scripturally represent His nature and character. This is certainly not the God revealed in Scripture.

Some "consistent" Calvinists make God the source of all evil and feel that somehow this solves the problem. But far from solving anything, it only compounds the problem making God both the author of all evil and the God who opposes it at the same time. This also entirely misrepresents His nature and character. For example, on John Piper's website (as of 2020) it says:

> God . . . brings about all things in accordance with his will. In other words, it isn't just that God manages to turn the evil aspects of our world to good for those who love him; it is rather that he himself brings about these evil aspects for his glory and his people's good. This includes—as incredible and as unacceptable as it may currently seem—God's having even brought about the Nazis' brutality at Birkenau and Auschwitz as well as the terrible killings of Dennis Rader and even the sexual abuse of a young child...[20]

Additionally, in an excerpt from a debate between Dr. James White (Calvinist) and George Bryson (non-Calvinist) on the Bible Answer Man broadcast, George Bryson asked James White:

> [Bryson] "When a child is raped, is God responsible and did He decree that rape?"

> [White] "If he didn't, then that rape is an element of meaningless evil that has no purpose. ...Yes. Because, if not, then it is meaningless and purposeless. And though God knew it was going to happen, he created it without a purpose. That means God brought the evil into existence, knowing it was going to exist, but for no purpose, no redemption, nothing positive, nothing good. ...Then every rape, every situation like that is nothing but purposeless evil, and God is responsible for the despair."

> [Bryson] "...God can use evil, and he does. But to blame God, which is what a decree does, to blame God for the rape of a child is a horrible attack on the very character and love of God."[21]

Still, other Calvinists try to avoid this dilemma by claiming that there is a mystery to all this and classify themselves as "compatibilists." Compatibilism teaches that man's moral freedom is "compatible" with God's determinism. In other words, how can God determine all acts—including man's decisions—and still have a person morally responsible for their choices? "The compatibilist view is that when man hears the call of the gospel, he is only free to reject the gospel unless God regenerates him; if God regenerates him, he is only free to accept the gospel, which he will do without exception."[22] According to Calvinists themselves:

> Compatibilism (also known as soft determinism), is the belief that God's predetermination and meticulous providence is "compatible" with voluntary choice. In light of Scripture, human choices are believed to be exercised voluntarily but the desires and circumstances that bring

about these choices occur through divine determinism (see Acts 2:23 & 4:27-28). It should be noted that this position is no less deterministic than hard determinism - be clear that neither soft nor hard determinism believes man has a free will. Our choices are only our choices because they are voluntary, not coerced. We do not make choices contrary to our desires or natures. Compatibilism is directly contrary to libertarian free will. Therefore voluntary choice is not the freedom to choose otherwise, that is, without any influence, prior prejudice, inclination, or disposition. Voluntary does mean, however, the ability to choose what we want or desire most. The former view is known as contrary choice, the latter free agency. (Note: compatibilism denies that the will is free to choose otherwise, that is, free from the bondage of the corruption nature, for the unregenerate, and denies that the will is free from God's eternal decree.)[23]

Since there is no way to understand how God can determine all things and allow human freedom, many Calvinists appeal to mystery as the solution. However, the Bible does not call this a mystery and therefore lacks justification to make this appeal. The biblical writers assume that people have actual choices that in fact could have been decided otherwise. This is how the writers penned the Scriptures. To rewrite it removes the obvious meaning the Holy Spirit conveyed very clearly in words. Indeed, the Holy Spirit provides anthropomorphisms to describe certain characteristics of God in human terms for our understanding. But this is because God wants His word and descriptions of Him understood in the simplest and clearest manner. The last thing that the Scriptures, or God, does is intentionally deceive or misguide through what is written. That would undermine the entire purpose of the Scriptures themselves and fly in the face of what Jesus said, "Thy word is truth" (John 17:17).

A note about Calvinistic compatibilism is important at this juncture. Compatibilism can be compared to asking a person appearing on a game show, who has the ability to see only black and white colors (all other colors being invisible to them) to choose the red door for an opportunity to win the million dollar prize. Since they cannot see the red door, they will never choose it. After failing to select the red door that they cannot see, they are informed that they had their opportunity, but unfortunately cannot continue in the game and are eliminated. What kind of game show would eliminate contestants unfairly? In the same way, compatibilists believe the elimination of the "non-elect" is accomplished. Though the "non-elect" are never given faith as a gift to believe, Calvinists believe they are still responsible for their decisions because they are making them freely, which means they make them according to their desires from their unregenerate nature. However, they are never provided the enablement through regeneration (according to the Calvinist view) to actually make a choice for Christ, since the only way that occurs under Calvinism is when God regenerates them first. Therefore, though Calvinists "speak" in terms of human responsibility, the reprobate is never given an actual opportunity to make a choice *for* Christ, no different from the game show contestant who is blind to the red door. Choices can only be free decisions if the person is able to choose other than what they actually do choose. If they can only make one decision regarding salvation because the "other" decision is hidden from or unavailable to them, they are not actually free, nor should be responsible. This distorts both the nature and character of God since God makes it clear that He holds man responsible for their decisions. In fact, God will judge both believers and unbelievers for their choices, believers regarding reward (2 Cor. 5:10), unbelievers regarding eternal damnation (Rev. 20:12). In each case, the Scriptures make it clear that the individual makes the choices freely, which is why God judges accordingly.

If a Calvinist tries to make the case that man is responsible for their sin and deserves God's wrath because of their sin, though true, there is one thing they should remember. God is the one who declares His justice and righteousness in His dealings with man. God is the one that pleads with the sinner and says He does not want to judge (Ezek. 18), and wills their repentance (2 Peter 3:9). Therefore, we can take the Scriptures as written and believe them. Indeed, no amount of philosophical determinism can make this verse coherent, "They have built also the high places of Baal, to burn their sons with fire for burnt offerings unto Baal, which I commanded not, nor spake it, neither came it into my mind" (Jer. 19:5). How could the wicked practices of idolatry that God is condemning through Jeremiah be something He determined if their actions never even came into His mind? Calvinists believe that God cannot foreknow something He does not determine. They believe that God knows the future because He determines it. Which means that the only way He could know that these idolaters in Jeremiah's day would commit wickedness would be to determine it. Yet, if that were the case, it would have come into His mind. Indeed, it would have not only come into His mind, but it would have to be something He willed for them to do because He determined them to do it. This perspective maintains a consistent Calvinism, but is highly inconsistent with and opposite to the perspective of the Bible.

Ronnie Rogers, a pastor who abandoned Calvinism after twelve years of thoroughly investigating it, observes: "Non-Calvinists believe that God created man in his image, which includes man having libertarian free choice. Creating man in the image of God necessarily includes the ability to choose other than he did in fact choose; he could act or refrain."[24] This is the fundamental difference between the theology of Calvinism and non-Calvinist orthodox theologies. The Bible teaches that man is responsible for the decision regarding faith in Christ. Therefore, to impose responsibly without providing an opportunity to choose other than the choice they in fact make presents a God that is unjust according to His own standards by violating them. First, God issues commands (Gen. 2:17; Exodus 20, 10 commandments; Acts 17:30; a few examples), which from a

Calvinistic perspective, man is incapable of choosing to obey unless God enables them. An interesting example in this regard is found under the law. God says by way of command to the Israelites, "Thou shalt not curse the deaf, nor put a stumblingblock before the blind, but shalt fear thy God: I am the LORD" (Lev. 19:14). Why would God command His people to avoid putting a stumbling block in front of a physically blind person (which seems self-evident to avoid such cruelty), and then judge people that are spiritually blind (those in need of redemption) due to no fault of their own? The commands in the Bible express God's nature; they are not capricious or arbitrary. In the Lev. 19:14 command, God would not act in such a cruel manner; thus, He wants His people to avoid such cruelty to blind people since they represent Him. The statement at the end of the verse implies this representative aspect, "fear thy God: I am the LORD," but commands one to assume personal responsibility. Unfortunately, when Calvinists ascribe to compatibilism, what they appear to forget is that God determines even the decisions of an unregenerate person making a choice based on their nature; it is inescapable. Why would God command His people to do anything and judge them when they do not obey, especially when He can determine that they do obey? If it were rebutted that He can justly judge them if they do not obey, that question assumes that the person is free in their decision to obey or not to obey, which conflicts with determinism. Either way, this passage and many others make no sense within a Calvinistic framework, which is the point. Therefore, there is nothing "compatible" with determinism, and appealing to human desire does not change that fact. On the contrary, in an attempt to avoid the deterministic conflict and appeal to a view more palatable, Calvinists have not solved anything; they have created an additional problem. Determinism is an absolute control of all decisions, so to fantasize of some amount of freedom in human decisions under this logically contradictory philosophy creates a conflict with determinism that is unsolvable. But then again, this is the continual abuse of logic and reason we see Calvinists

REDISCOVERING ROMANS 9

argue from consistently, while at the same time, they attempt to use logic and reason to defend their system. This is a logical conflict Calvinists remain blind to, so if we use their reasoning process, apparently God determined they remain blind in this area.

43

RESPONSE TO UNCONDITIONAL ELECTION

This is the real linchpin to the Calvinistic system. Without this piece, the system entirely fails. As far as Calvinists are concerned, God makes all the choices of who the saved will be and who the lost will be by eternal decree prior to a person's existence, that God predestined some to everlasting life (the elect) and others to everlasting destruction (the reprobate).[25] They believe that any decision on man's part is some form of human merit—-this includes faith when viewed in a free will context![26] They believe if God allows a person to exercise "their own faith" that there is some aspect of human merit in that exercise, and God is no longer sovereign. In that case, God ultimately becomes submissive to man's decision, or man becomes the sovereign in the salvation process. Thus, as far as Calvinists are concerned, there is no condition knowable to man regarding God's choice of an individual person to salvation or damnation prior to their existence. But, in Calvinism, if a person cannot respond to the gospel and believe, even through the convicting work of the Holy Spirit, in essence God must do the believing for them (Irresistible Grace), or make them believe. I know many Calvinists do not like that statement and feel it misrepresents their system, but in effect, if the person cannot exercise their own belief, then God is not just *enabling* them to believe, but *ensuring* they will believe! This is because God will irresistibly overwhelm them with His grace and cause them to believe; there is no option. Therefore, God is the one that makes the choice for them from eternity and irresistibly infuses them with spiritual life so they *will* believe. They believe God's will overrides man's will; therefore, He is making them believe or in essence, believing for them since they cannot do it on their own (more on this under Irresistible Grace). Bottom line, since man is so dead in his fallen state that he cannot respond—even to God—election of those whom God will save must occur before the individual is ever born. How do Calvinists know there is no condition upon which God chooses some to salvation? They logically deduce it from their definition of Total Depravity (or Inability). Man in Calvinistic thinking will never be able to respond to anything God puts in front of him; thus, God must choose them and infuse them with spiritual life first. Since man has no condition to fulfill, especially since before they are born God makes the decision, Calvinists classify the choice as without condition or unconditional. There is no Bible verse that spells out this scenario, nor is it developed anywhere in the Bible. It is the logical construct of Calvin's theology into the T.U.L.I.P. acronym.

Whenever I talk to a person making a life-changing decision to follow Calvinist teachings, if they allow me, I ask how they understand them. If they understand what the 5 Points are, I ask if they can explain them. The range of responses makes it clear that many make the decision on some factor other than a proper understanding of Calvinism. One young man, who decided to leave our church for this reason, provides a good example of how people who seem to understand and articulate certain aspects of the teachings do not. In our conversation, the young man stated to the best of my recollection, "I have never understood God's love for me as I have since I believed unconditional election and realized that God by His eternal decree elected me to salvation." At that point, I realized he really had very little understanding of Calvinism or the Bible for that fact. He may have memorized the 5 Points, but he poured his *own* perspective into Calvin's doctrine. This is a common problem among Christians in general, not just Calvinists. Too often, Christians adhere to certain beliefs for a myriad of reasons other than the doctrinal positions themselves. In the case of this young man, two things clearly escaped his notice. *First*, he understood God's love based on the fact that God elected him to salvation. The problem with his perspective is that unconditional election is not based on love for the individual in the sense that it is some condition in the individual causing God's choice. Since it is not based on any knowable condition—at least not one that is knowable to man—to assume that God made the choice of an individual based on anything in the individual is contrary to the doctrine itself. Calvinists assume that God's love is the basis of election, certainly an enjoyable position for the elect. However, it does not mention that God elects anyone based on love. God's love is why He sent Christ to redeem the world (John 3:16). Therefore, this young man was ascribing to God a reason for God's choosing him that is not part of the Calvinistic system. Yet he found great comfort in his misunderstanding of Calvinism; he simply adjusted the system to his own comfort. Calvinists frequently talk about God's *special* love to the "elect," but how do they establish that when the "election" has no condition knowable to them? To claim election is based on love establishes a condition in an unconditional system. Indeed, the Bible is very clear that God not only loves His people, but the whole world, the saved and unsaved (John 3:16). But even this is contrary to the teaching of unconditional election. Calvinists distinguish God's love creating a contrast between the elect and the non-elect. This is not based on a clear teaching in the Bible; it is the logical deduction of what they observe operationally in the world. Since they believe God loves and atones for the elect only, they conclude that the non-elect cannot enjoy the same level of love from God; otherwise, they would be the elect. It is a conclusion tightly coupled to the T.U.L.I.P. system to maintain its logical coherence. Or, as noted above, they reason in a circle, assuming what they are trying to prove. *Second*, the cross is the focus of the Bible when describing God's love for man. Love for the world finds its source in God, not anything in man. This is why His love is unalterable since it is grounded in God, not in man. This love is the motivation of His grace and acts of mercy to the sinner. Moreover, God's love is grounded in His nature (1 John 4:8), not that He has more love than man does (though He of course does), but His nature defines or embodies the definition of love. We observe God expressing His nature of love in man's redemption through Christ. Therefore, it is from the cross that we receive assurance of that love (Rom. 5:8), *not* from election. The purpose of election is entirely different (God's purpose in election is discussed below in the Roman's 9 exposition). In Calvinism (at least philosophically and among many of the modern Calvinists), the cross is almost incidental. Accordingly, God is determined to save people by His decree, which is the basis of their system resulting in their undue focus on election. To be one of the elect is like winning the eternal lottery, and from man's perspective, it is just as arbitrary. When it comes to the cross in Calvinism, it is like a cog in the wheel of the salvation process to fulfill the divine decree. However, the Bible does not describe the cross in that way. The cross is the very epicenter of man's salvation; it is where the entire payment for our sins took place (John 19:30) and the very act of our redemption. The OT looks forward to the cross and the NT looks back at it. I discover the love, grace, and mercy of God through it and nothing else is comparable to it. Jesus and the prophets emphasized it ahead of time and the apostles reemphasized it afterward. Nowhere is a divine decree of unconditional election the basis of our worship or the means of our salvation. No prophet speaks of it, and neither Jesus nor the apostles emphasize it as the reason for our salvation.

Getting back to the young man in my example, it was unfortunate he was so thrilled with what he felt Calvinism did for him. Though he understood what the 5 Points were, he evidently did not understand the theological implications of them. His security was in a philosophically flawed system of determinism which he redefined and misunderstood. He is a perfect example of why this whole system of Calvinism is problematic. This example only begins to unravel the almost countless contradictions and problems within the framework of the Calvinistic world.

Contrary to this view of unconditional election, the Bible provides us information regarding God's election of people in reference to salvation; however, it is associated with the faith of the individual and their response in time. In other words, election is "according to the foreknowledge of God the Father" (1 Peter 1:2). *Foreknowledge* is an attribute of God's omniscience.[27] It is not—according to the claim of Calvinists—foreordination or predestination. In that case, it would change from an attribute to an act and a different word would have described it. God decided His eternal plan of salvation before He created man; He chose (elected) a specific plan to be accomplished in the precise manner aligned with His purposes in grace. In Rev. 13:8, it says, "And all that dwell upon the earth shall worship him [the Beast], whose names are not written in the book of life of the Lamb slain from the foundation of the world." Regardless of your particular eschatology, there is at least one thing clear in this verse that is beyond dispute, "the Lamb slain from the foundation of the world." The redemptive plan of God was not an afterthought (1Cor. 2:7: Titus 1:2; 1 Peter 1:20). God knew from the "foundation of the world" that He would send His Son to pay the price for the sin of the world (John 1:29); this is reflected in Peter's sermon in Acts 2:23. God *knows* all that will (or potentially could) occur in time, and He knows it all at once in eternity past. God cannot learn anything. He knows all that is knowable; therefore, He can reveal the future through prophets. The future is not really the future for God since He sees all time in the present. Prophecy is exciting for us because it occurs in time and we watch it unfold, but for God, He just reveals history in advance since He sees it all. It glorifies God and causes us to marvel at His majesty.

As mentioned, Peter associates election with God's foreknowledge in 1 Peter 1:2. Thus, God revealed His plan to us in Scripture along with the condition required to apply that work of Christ to us personally. What is that condition? It is the humility of true faith. We are told that God resists the proud but gives grace to the humble (Psalm 34:18, 51:17; Isaiah 57:15, 66:2; Matt. 5:3; Luke 14:11; James 4:6; 1 Peter 5:5), a principle that is a constant theme of Scripture. I am *not* saying that people earn grace; what I am saying is there is a condition necessary for receiving the grace offered. That receptive aspect in a person is not a work; it is simply the faith to receive the gift of salvation. That kind of humble reception is necessary to receive the salvation of God. We receive it with empty hands; we have nothing to offer God. As Toplady wrote in his hymn:

> Nothing in my hand I bring,
>
> Simply to the cross I cling;
>
> Naked, come to thee for dress;
>
> Helpless, look to thee for grace.[28]

The Holy Spirit convicts all and draws all to Christ (John 12:32, 16:8), but only those who humbly receive Him will respond in faith and believe (Acts 28:23-28). The quote from Isaiah 6:9-10 (Isaiah's commission by God) is referenced a number of times in the NT (Matt. 13:14-15; Mark 4:12; Luke 8:10; John 12:40; Acts 28:26-27; 2 Cor. 3:14-15). Unfortunately, Calvinists have understood this passage as God determinatively hardening certain people before they were born in reference to His choice of who He will and will not save. First, a simple reading of Isaiah's commission will dispel that view (Isaiah 6:1-10). If you read the next verses (Isaiah 6:11-13), it reveals that the commission is prophetic and Isaiah was to continue in answer to his question "Lord, how long?". The answer was until judgment came on the nation. Israel would continue to rebel and reject Isaiah's preaching, but his commission was to be obedient regardless of results. God was giving Israel time to repent; however, they would continue down their rebellious road of idolatry to judgment and their exile to Babylon.

This prophetic commission of Isaiah indicated what Israel *would* do in light of Isaiah's message, not what God *made* them do. Isaiah's ministry and lack of positive response from the nation was prophetic of what God *knew*, not deterministic of what God *ordained*. God's foreknowing is not God's determining. Remember, God's foreknowledge is one of His attributes; it is not an action. Determining is an ordaining action that makes something occur. Nonetheless, God continued to hold out His hand to Israel and desired their repentance, but they would not. "I have spread out my hands all the day unto a rebellious people, which walketh in a way that was not good, after their own thoughts" (Isaiah 65:2). Interesting that this verse emphasizes that Israel's rebellion was "after their own thoughts," not thoughts that God determinatively gave them. If God determined that Israel would reject Him, He would be in conflict with His own word (Isaiah 1:16-21; 65:2). He would have been hardening them on the one hand and reaching out to them on the other. Why would we interpret the Scriptures to make God look like He is in this self-conflict? It distorts His nature and brings question to His character.

Similarly, Moses' commission to go to Egypt contains a prophetic aspect. He was told ahead of time (prophetically) how Pharaoh would respond (Ex. 4:21). However, God was not determining Pharaoh's response; God knew how he would respond (there is nothing God does not know). God knew that when Moses gave the message to release Israel, Pharaoh would not accommodate it. This initially resulted in Pharaoh's own self-hardening through his own continued resistance. Therefore, Pharaoh—as the Scripture describes—initially hardened his own heart (Ex. 7:14, 22; 8:15, 19, 32; 9:34-35). However, God used that hardening to accomplish His redemptive plan with His people. Pharaoh's hard heart was eventually made firm by God's hardening it, but only after Pharaoh continued to reject the demands. In other words, Pharaoh's hardening was the result of the continued interchange with Moses. But make no mistake, though God was in control of the entire process; God did not determine the entire process; Pharaoh's rejection was his own. God determined to release His people and judge Egypt (Gen. 15:13-14) because He knew the course of events and how the future would proceed, hence the prophecy. There is a mixture throughout the Scriptures of God accomplishing His determined redemptive plan through the nation and the free will of the people involved. Moreover, this is similar to Paul's exchange in Acts 26:23-28, where he tried all day to convince the Jews of the gospel of Jesus Christ. But in the end, most turned away. He then quoted from Isaiah 6:9-10 to them (our passage under consideration) because they fulfilled the same hardhearted conditions as their ancestors. Paul's usage of the Isaiah 6:9-10 reference was not deterministic; to interpret it that way robs the context and nullifies the reason and force behind Paul's quoting it. Indeed, only when the Isaiah passage is frontloaded with Calvinistic presuppositions will a deterministic interpretation be the conclusion.

What is interesting about Calvin's view on *unconditional* election is that he seemed to know somewhat of the *conditions* for it. Logically, to know someone makes a choice unconditionally, what must be known is the reason for the choice; otherwise, the choice appears capricious or arbitrary. On the other hand, if the reason is not declared for the choice, everything about the one making the choice must be known to conclude the reason is with or without condition. In other words, there is required knowledge about God to conclude He is making an unconditional election. But within Calvinism, this knowledge of the reason God elects is not available. When it comes to God, the Bible does not tell us that He made a choice to save some unconditionally and damn others, which requires Calvinistic frontloading. We also cannot know everything about

God; only what He reveals about Himself in Scripture. For "the Bible is not a revelation of what God knows, but what God wants us to know."[29] Thus, we must take what is written, and base our understanding on that truth. Yet Calvin built an entire theology around *how*, *when*, and *who* God would elect. Yet He could not tell *why* God would choose them on the one hand, but tells us it was *unconditional* on the other. His explanation surrounds the sovereign will of God alone as the determination for the choice, but how can he know that if the Bible does not reveal it? Moreover, he claims God's decisions to save some and not others is not arbitrary or capricious, but how can he know this? Therefore, Calvin assigns the condition as none, but cannot tell us why or where it actually says that in Scripture. He concludes that there is no condition man possesses for God to "elect" him and reasons the election is unconditional. But it is a far stretch to conclude that because there is no *merit* in man for him to be saved, there is no *condition* required in man to be saved. The two are not equal.

The irony is, the Bible does tell us *why* some are saved and others are not; it is part of the fabric of Scripture. God saves by grace because He loves by nature, and the requirement for receiving His redemption is faith. It is not complicated, for God kept it simple and comprehendible. God's entire redemptive plan and process fills in the why, with man's faith as the receptive condition to be part of that plan. If God did not disclose this for us in Scripture, we would not know how salvation took place at all. Calvinism leaves us in a quandary, having no indication of who or why God would save. God saves those who respond by faith and He does it because it is His plan of redemption expressed in the gospel. Yet, this one aspect of the Bible that need not be confusing or complicated by imposing Calvinistic determinism on it. What Calvinists seem to miss is that their system is deterministic regarding their view of God Himself and they have determined how God must act to maintain His sovereignty. Ironically, they sovereignly declare

He can only save the way they have reasoned. Indeed, this is a dangerous role reversal of who is the decision maker in this scenario. This perspective maintained by most Calvinists is in direct opposition to their aggressive campaign for maintaining God's sovereignty—as they determine it must operate. This perspective certainly does not glorify God, though God's glory is paramount in Calvinistic theology. The irony is conspicuous.

RESPONSE TO LIMITED ATONEMENT

Calvinists believe that the atonement of Christ was only for the elect. It is the logical consequence of unconditional election; the ones that God elected are the only ones Jesus atoned for. In their view, the person Jesus atones for must be a redeemed person since they have atonement for their sins. In other words, how can Jesus pay for the sins of someone and they still possess their sins? However, to understand the distinctions properly, *limited* atonement holds that Jesus died for the elect, where *unlimited* atonement (not universalism that holds everyone is automatically saved) holds that Jesus died for everyone. Limited atonement holds that all whom Christ died for will be saved, where unlimited atonement holds that though Christ died for all, not all will be saved.

The question naturally arises regarding the applicability of unlimited atonement. Unlimited atonement holds that Jesus atoned for everyone, which means everyone is savable. However, regarding unlimited atonement, a person is not born again until they believe in Jesus. In 1 John 2:2 it says, "And he is the propitiation for our sins: and not for ours only, but also for the sins of the whole world." The word *propitiation* simply means satisfaction, that Jesus' sacrifice satisfied the just demands of a Holy God on behalf of all sinners. Thus, Christ paid the sin debt of the world--removed the sin barrier between God and man--leaving man the responsibility to believe by their own free will. Therefore, it is not just the offer of salvation to all, which Calvinists would accept, though not all are savable in their view. It is the payment for all, which makes everyone savable. Unlimited atonement holds that everyone's sins were atoned for at the cross and God's righteous demands are satisfied. This includes the OT saints who died in faith prior to the actual work of the cross in time. Paul said, "God set forth as a propitiation by His blood, through faith, to demonstrate His righteousness, because in His forbearance God had passed over the sins that were previously committed, to demonstrate at the present time His righteousness, that He might be just and the justifier of the one who has faith in Jesus" (Rom. 3:25-26, NKJV). These "[s]ins *done aforetime* are the collective sins of the world before Christ."[30]

No one can be saved apart from the work of Jesus Christ on the cross, and this includes infants and the mentally incompetent. Though a different subject than what we are now discussing, the theological principle here is crucial. The only way infants and the mentally incompetent benefit from Christ's atonement, since they cannot personally apply it, is if everyone is under the atonement of Christ. God requires those who possess understanding the exercise of faith, as Paul clearly teaches in Romans 3. However, the mere fact that the atonement of Jesus covers all the sins of people before Christ's redeeming sacrifice on the cross informs us that the atonement is not limited only to the "elect." For the OT saints are not "elect" in the same equal sense as are the NT saints. The election in the context of the OT relates to corporate national Israel, not individuals. This is the point Paul emphasizes in the first part of Romans 9. God chose Israel as a national ethnic group and gifted them with special benefits as His chosen people, but "they are not all Israel, which are of Israel" (Rom. 9:6). In other words, not everyone in the nation possessed faith and believed. Therefore, the Calvinist cannot ever know what infant or mentally incompetent person is one of the "elect" if the atonement is limited, for there is no means of evaluation of their faith in Christ. Since infants and mentally incompetent people cannot exercise genuine faith in Christ on their own, Calvinists have concocted various and sundry rituals and methods to make sure those in these vulnerable conditions somehow get to heaven. Unfortunately, it is never a scripturally sound solution, but normally tied to some former Calvinist of the Reformation period that utilized infant baptism or some other human invention. This is why God made Christ the propitiation for the sins of the whole world because God knew what He was doing. Thus, the world is atoned for and now the gospel is the message to be reconciled to God (2 Cor. 5:20). Other than the infant and mentally incompetent, salvation comes to the sinner when they believe in Jesus Christ; God then gives them eternal life. In this way, all those saved come through the cross of Christ. There is no other way! This is why the cross is the epicenter of God's redemptive plan--and what a marvelous plan it is!

It would be hard to imagine that those who hold to limited and unlimited atonement can both read the same Bible and come to such opposite conclusions. However, this is the result of defining words in the Bible differently than the context or the very definition of that word itself requires. Frontloading Calvinistic views into the words in these limited atonement "proof texts" can yield some bizarre conclusions. For example, in John 3:16, the word "world" is not believed by Calvinists to mean what it normally does in other verses or its evident context. Reading the verse without any Calvinistic preconditioning would tell us that God loves everyone in the *world*. In this case, unlimited atonement would hold that, "it means that He loves every person, head for head, equally."[31] However, within the limited atonement camp, this is not a logical—though it is biblical—conclusion. "The logic goes something like this: God loves every person; Christ died for every person; therefore, salvation is possible for every person. However, this view seems to suggest that God's love is impotent and Christ's death is ineffectual. Otherwise, the natural conclusion of this position would be that every person is actually saved rather than just potentially saved. If God loves every person, and Christ died for every person, and God's love is not impotent, and Christ's death is not ineffectual, then the only conclusion one can draw is that salvation has been secured for every person."[32] Therefore, their Calvinistic presuppositions cause them to conflate the *work* of Christ and the *application* of salvation without separating the need for man's free choice in the process. In other words, those paid for on the cross will have salvation applied to them; it is not within the possibility of alteration since the "elect" are not making any free will decisions in the process. This deterministic framework used by Calvinists to interpret the Bible causes them to draw this conclusion. Calvinists therefore do not differentiate between the work of Jesus' atonement and the application of it to the individual. To them, the work of Christ on the cross is automatically applied to those elected--end of story. Calvinists do not believe they receive Jesus' atonement by active faith, but they are in fact passive in the reception of redemption because of God's deterministic application of the atonement to them. This is why they must limit the atonement to those elected without any known condition, leaving all others without atonement passed over to damnation.

The Bible tells us a very different story. Let's return to John 3:16 for a closer look. First, "God so loved the world that He gave His only begotten Son, that whoever believes in Him should not perish but have everlasting life." John's reference to the "world" (Gk. *kosmos*), is not "the elect" nor is His love redefined to mean that there is a quality of God's love Calvinists claim He has for only "the elect." They understand God loves the elect as normally stated in Scripture, but for the non-elect, there is a lesser quality of love, since there is no salvation available for them. But the verse says God loves all, since the world consists of everyone in it. Moreover, this offer is to "whoever," which means anyone; there is no limit in the verse describing God's love or the world. John uses the word "world" 79 times in 58 verses and it never has the interpretation that Calvinists try to squeeze into it in 3:16. No one reading the gospel of John would naturally conclude a limited atonement that Calvinists thrust on particular passages.

Using this definition of the word "world" accords with the rest of the NT; a few passages should suffice. John in his first epistle, using the same word for "world" tells us that Jesus' propitiation was sufficient for everyone, though efficient for those who believe. "And he is the propitiation for our sins: and not for ours only, but also for the sins of the whole world" (1 John 2:2). John obviously differentiates believers from unbelievers contrasting "ours" from the "whole world." Paul is also in agreement, for in 1 Tim. 2:5 he states that God "desires all men to be saved and to come to the knowledge of the truth" (NKJV). Peter in his second epistle by implication states the atonement is evidently unlimited, else, how could it involve "false teachers?" He says, "But there were also false prophets among the people, even as there will be false teachers among you, who will secretly bring in destructive heresies, even denying the Lord who bought them, and bring on themselves swift destruction" (2 Peter 2:1, NKJV). Thus, the atonement must be unlimited, encompassing the entire human race. Finally, in Hebrews 2:9 it says, "But we see Jesus, who was made a little lower than the angels for the suffering of death, crowned with glory and honour; that he by the grace of God should taste death for every man." This verse is so clear, I hesitate to comment on it lest I detract from its impact! The following verses also speak of unlimited atonement; however, comments are not necessary since the verses speak for themselves:

"Behold the Lamb of God, which taketh away the sin of the world" (John 1:29).

"For the bread of God is he which cometh down from heaven, and giveth life unto the world" (John 6:33).

"I am the living bread which came down from heaven: if any

man eat of this bread, he shall live for ever: and the bread that I will give is my flesh, which I will give for the life of the world" (John 6:51).

"And I, if I be lifted up from the earth, will draw all men unto me" (John 12:32).

"Therefore as by the offence of one judgment came upon all men to condemnation; even so by the righteousness of one the free gift came upon all men unto justification of life" (Rom. 5:18).

"God was in Christ, reconciling the world unto himself, not imputing their trespasses unto them" (2 Cor. 5:19).

"For the grace of God that bringeth salvation hath appeared to all men" (Titus 2:11).

"And we have seen and do testify that the Father sent the Son to be the Saviour of the world" (1 John 4:14).

It is impossible to remain honest with the text and change any of these to fit the limited atonement view. Unfortunately, Calvinistic commentators go through some fancy literary contortions to squeeze their limited atonement views into these and other texts. Like the old saying goes, "if you torture a text long enough you can get it to say anything."[33] I believe the Bible has been tortured far too long, forcing it to cry out contrary to what the text naturally says which the Holy Spirit inspired the authors to pen. If anything needs to be limited, it is the torture of these, or any other texts by Calvinists.[34]

Indeed, changing the meaning of the salvation offered by Jesus and the apostles by infusing preloaded Calvinistic philosophical concepts is the only way to conclude a limited atonement. However, when this is done, God's nature and character is distorted by making God's salvation offer disingenuous and deceptive. If there are two things that have nothing to do with God's holy nature and perfect character, it is disingenuousness and deceptiveness. The following chart correlates some texts that follow the same line of presentation;

the salvation God provided is objectively accomplished for all and is subjectively appropriated to those who believe. As Meyer commenting on 2 Cor. 5:19, (the first example in the following chart):

> [κόσμον] not *a* world, but *the* world, even without the article (Winer, p. 117 [E. T. 153]), as Gal. 6:14; Rom. 4:13. It applies to *the whole human race*, not possibly (in opposition to Augustine, Lyra, Beza, Cajetanus, Estius) merely to those *predestinated*. The reconciliation *of all men* took place objectively through Christ's death, although the subjective appropriation of it is conditioned by the faith of the individual.[35]

Atonement Chart

TEXT	UNIVERSAL OFFER (*SUFFICIENT* FOR ALL)	CONDITION OF ACCEPTANCE (*EFFICIENT* FOR THOSE WHO BELIEVE)
2 Cor. 5:19-20	God was in Christ, reconciling the **world** unto himself	be **ye** reconciled to God
John 1:9, 12	This [Lit. He] was the true light that **enlightens every person** by his coming into the **world**. (ISV)	to **all who received him**, those **believing** in his name, he gave authority to become God's children (ISV)
John 3:16	God so loved the **world** that He gave His only begotten Son	**whosoever believeth** in him should not perish, but have everlasting life
John 6:33, 35	The bread of God is He which cometh down from heaven, and giveth life unto the **world**.	he that **cometh** to me shall never hunger; and he that **believeth** on me shall never thirst.
John 6:51	The bread that I will give is My flesh, which I will give for the life of the **world**.	if **any man eat** of this bread, he shall live for ever:
Mark 16:15-16	As you go into **all the world**, proclaim the gospel to **everyone**. [Lit. to the whole creation] (ISV)	**Whoever believes** and is baptized will be saved, but whoever **doesn't believe** will be condemned. (ISV)
1 Tim. 2:3-4,6	God our Savior, since he **wants all people** to be saved and to come to a knowledge of the truth. ...who gave himself as a **ransom for all** (NET)	**Saved** [by faith, Eph. 2:8] and to come to a knowledge of the truth
1 Tim. 4:10	we trust in the living God, who is the **Savior of all men** (NKJV)	especially of those who **believe**. (NKJV)
Titus 2:11, 14	the grace of God has appeared, bringing salvation **for all people** (ESV)	Who gave himself **for us**, **that he might redeem us** [who believe]
Heb. 2:9, 13	he [Jesus] by the grace of God should taste death **for every man**.	I will put my **trust** in him.
2 Peter 2:1	disowning even the Sovereign Lord who **has redeemed them** [false teachers] and bringing on themselves swift [eternal] destruction. (WNT)	there will be teachers of falsehood among **you** [believers] (WNT)
1 John	he himself is the atoning	he himself is the atoning

2:2	*sacrifice for our sins, and not only for our sins but also for the **whole world**. (ISV)*	*sacrifice **for our [believers] sins**, and not only for our sins but also for the whole world. (ISV)*

RESPONSE TO IRRESISTIBLE GRACE

Irresistible grace is next in our logical system of 5-Point Calvinism. The connection should be clear; if dead people cannot respond to the gospel they must be unconditionally elected (since there is no condition in man under which they can believe). They alone are atoned for by the sacrifice of Christ and God will then irresistibly cause them to believe. The Calvinists like the phrase "make willing" or "change of disposition of man's will." However, we need to be clear about what this doctrine actually teaches, regardless of their more palatable terminology. It is not that people "might" believe, but they "will" believe—God has determined it because they are one of the "elect." Therefore, grace is not resistible and there is no other "option" for them.

Though the term irresistible sounds quite odd when combined with grace, nonetheless, it is the proper Calvinistic terminology. When we think of God's grace, since it provides benefits we are not deserving of, the forceful thought of irresistibility does not seem to align with the biblical idea of grace. We normally understand grace as a sister term to mercy and coupled with God's love. Paul in the context of a passage expressing these ideas said, "But God, who is rich in mercy, for his great love wherewith he loved us, Even when we were dead in sins, hath quickened us together with Christ, (by grace ye are saved)" (Eph. 2:5). Therefore, we did not fall under God's judgment, which we deserved since "we were dead in sins," but instead received His mercy. God is "rich in mercy" since our sin demands the judgment of God—unless there is an option

—which God provided in the redemptive work of Christ which enabled us to be "quickened [made alive] together with Christ." It was God's "great love wherewith he loved us" that moved Him to send His Son. In addition, it is "by grace" we were saved. If God did not initiate His plan of redemption, no one could be saved. It is entirely due to the love, mercy, and grace of God that man can be saved; thus, to associate the graciousness of God to such a forceful term appears to be entirely out of character with the nature and character of God.

Calvinists typically respond negatively when their opponents claim their view is that man cannot resist God's grace. This is because their opponents believe there are clear instances in Scripture of man resisting God's grace. However, Calvinists believe in the *particular* case of regeneration that God is more powerful than man's resistance, or that God sovereignly overpowers man's nature causing him to believe. So there is clarity in what God accomplishes in the Calvinistic system, it is not that God eternally foreknows that the elect would believe in time, but He makes them believe in time. He does not draw them by His Spirit, but determines them by His power. This view is riddled with biblical complications, logical contradictions, and conflicting theological problems. However, for the sake of space a few points should suffice to make the case against irresistible grace.

As noted above, Calvinists, because of their presuppositions, must place regeneration prior to repentance. This is because in their view the only way a person will repent and believe in Christ is after they are made spiritually alive (regenerated) so they can then exercise faith; otherwise they are blind to their condition. Ephesians 2:1-8, clearly mishandled by Calvinists, becomes the ground for spiritual life irresistibly imposed before faith; however, even when faith is exercised it is not theirs alone. They claim God gives the gift of faith to the elect so they can then believe. I cited the classic Greek grammarians (experts in grammar) as proof that the verse cannot actually say what

Calvinists claim (that faith is the gift spoken of in Eph. 2:8). Thus, we must accept the facts even if they frustrate our desire for a particular biblical interpretation. This is proper whether Calvinist or non-Calvinist; we cannot ignore grammatical and contextual facts because they are found to refute a desired theological outcome.

The error in this case is reading the Bible through the lens of Calvinism instead of allowing the Bible to tell Calvinists what they should believe. Nevertheless, Calvinistic conclusions consistently take authority over the clear meaning of Scripture when there is a conflict, such as in Eph. 2:8. The other alternative, as unfavorable as this conclusion may be, is they are deliberately altering the text of Scripture to match their extreme fantasy of theological determinism. I would like to think that their unscriptural conclusion of Ephesians 2:8 is the result of ignorance or misguidance; however, among those more educated in biblical studies, I fear the unfavorable conclusion is more correct. Calvinists have mounted their efforts against this verse since its obvious meaning flies in the face of their doctrinal position. They must redefine it to align with their views or it will be the monkey wrench in the machinery of their theology. It would be one thing if the verse was vague or disputed, but in this case, they ignore the clear context and grammar. It is mystifying why they go to such lengths to maintain this loyalty to Calvin's theology. At a minimum, it calls into question their interpretive conclusions on other critical areas of Scripture. Will they simply alter the Bible to align with Calvin every time? Will they manipulate context and grammar when it suits them to produce a determinative theology (did God determine they would do this with His word)? Will they disregard the integrity of Scripture to maintain status among the Reformed community? Will they cherry-pick certain verses, ignoring those that contradict their views, in support of their preloaded Calvinistic conclusions? If history has given us any indication, I fear these questions are indeed rhetorical.

This is a very dangerous and deceptive method of Bible study. This practice has birthed many cults and heretical Bible teachings and should have no place within orthodox Christianity (I am not saying that Calvinism is a cult or that all their views are heretical). This problematic practice of Bible study hinders the church's attempt to use apologetics in a consistent manner to reach the world with the gospel, since they neutralize some very powerful biblical texts. The Calvinistic view on many of these Bible texts creates evangelistic problems that frankly do not need to exist. If Calvinism were true, it would be very difficult to give unbelievers a defense (GK. apologia) for the hope that lies within us. Peter said in 1 Peter 3:15, "in your hearts honor Christ the Lord as holy, always being prepared to make a defense to anyone who asks you for a reason for the hope that is in you; yet do it with gentleness and respect" (ESV). However, since it is not known whether or not the person asking is one of the elect, what hope can they reasonably offer with integrity and enthusiasm if they are the non-elect? What is the hope they can actually offer anyone? A Calvinist can perhaps offer the surety that they themselves are one of the elect by eternal decree, but that is not the gospel. The potential convert asking questions may not be one of the elect and this presents an operational difficulty for many Calvinists. Moreover, Calvinists tend to struggle (ethically within their doctrinal beliefs) presenting the gospel to groups or multitudes. They typically reject crusades or large groups since their theology tells them they may be offering the gospel to someone who may not be elect. This Calvinistic ethical dilemma is an unnecessary quandary and finds no support anywhere in the Bible. Imagine a crisis of conscience over whether or not to share the gospel with unbelievers—how crazy that sounds. Especially when the operational example we have in the Bible is abundantly clear; the offer of the gospel to both individuals and groups is an unmistakable pattern. We see Jesus and the apostles doing just that, so why should we do any different? *We shouldn't!*

If I have a problem offering the gospel to anyone with the "hope" that lies within me, something must be wrong. Only Calvinistic determinism would throw a monkey wrench in Peter's admonition (1 Peter 3:15). Calvinism does not provide anyone with actual hope, which by definition is contingent and conditional. The hope of the gospel is contingent upon my relationship with Christ, and that relationship is conditional upon my faith in Him. Imagine the honest presentation of the gospel by a Calvinist who actually understands Calvinism. "Hi, I would like to share that Jesus Christ may have died on the cross for your sins and redeemed you from an eternity in hell, but I'm not sure if you are one of the elect. If you are, God will irresistibly give you spiritual life at some point and cause you to believe. If you want to believe now, maybe that has already happened which would mean God regenerated you, meaning you are one of the elect. Once you make the step and believe in Jesus, you need to do good works. If you do, you will show you are one of the elect and have the assurance of salvation. The only ones that persevere until the end of their lives are the elect; the false believers fall away. Let me know if you are interested in becoming a Christian." What I left out in this theoretical Calvinistic gospel presentation was the Lordship Salvation that many Calvinists follow. But that would have complicated the offer to the extent that the entire presentation would be unrecognizable. The point is, a consistent Calvinist would have to over qualify and surround the simple gospel with all kinds of baggage and extras the Bible does not give us. Contrary to that reasoning, providing a "reason for the hope that lies within me" implies that a potential convert can use their own reasoning process (given by God) to evaluate the defense I am offering them to make a decision for Christ. Unfortunately in Calvinism, none of this applies and the verse becomes meaningless. Peter's statement only ostensibly applies to potential converts, but does not actually apply to them all. This only scratches the surface regarding the biblical, logical, and life application problems of irresistible grace.

Considering the theological (and logical) problem for a moment, this deterministic method of salvation removes the dignity of God and makes a mockery of the creation of man. Most Calvinists believe that when the gospel is preached to people, all are addressed outwardly (the gospel message heard with the physical ears), but only those who are the *elect* will be irresistibly given spiritual life (inwardly, termed "effectual calling" by Calvinists) so they will believe. This not only removes any freedom of the will God created man with, but also reduces man to a robot that is only doing exactly what God makes them to do. The tragedy of this theological perspective is that it is no different from the modern atheists that reject free will because of their materialistic presuppositions. In the end, the Calvinist makes God the cause of all man's decisions, where the atheist makes DNA the cause. Either way, in both beliefs, no one has a real choice to do anything they are not already made to do or caused to do. It is a form of unsupportable logical and biblical fatalism. I really have to chuckle when I hear this type of stuff from either Calvinists or atheists. They make many decisions freely that result in a self-determined system of contradictions that they purposely—and freely I might add—avoid. It is similar to when a Jehovah's Witness shows up on your doorstep. When you give them a verse that plainly contradicts their beliefs, they quickly, and freely, move to another topic and readjust their argument. But they never actually answer the question; avoidance is the main method with cults. The atheist uses the freedom of their consciousness, logic, reason, and philosophical arguments (all non-material aspects of man that cannot exist in their worldview) to argue against the existence of the non-material aspects of man. Similarly, the Calvinist uses their free will to make cases and argue against people that are not Calvinists—who apparently believe differently by God's eternal decree according to their view—thus they actually end up arguing against God! In other words, think of it this way: if God wanted me to be a Calvinist, I would be one (according to their deterministic view). If I have no free will, apparently I am writing this book because God has determined it, and interestingly enough, it is against Calvinistic views. Therefore, no Calvinist should object to anything I write, since God apparently predestined me by His determinism to write it. So a consistent Calvinist should fully agree with everything everyone claims, no matter how contradictory or unbiblical it is. Because in the end, they will find themselves arguing against God's determinative will. As I said above, Calvinism is riddled with so many biblical complications, logical contradictions, and conflicting theological problems, it would take a much larger work to fully address them. How could this theology possibly reveal an omniscient God of eternal wisdom? Certainly not by developing a system of theology where God is playing both sides of the chessboard and fighting against Himself at every turn. Irresistible grace is a perfect example of how Calvinism distorts the nature and character of God.

Moreover, Calvinists believe that if God is not controlling every detail of everything, He is not sovereign. However, in making the case that God cannot be sovereign unless He controls every minute detail of everyone and deterministically fixes what everyone will do etc., they are limiting God's sovereignty to their own definition of it. The Bible tells us God is infinite, all knowing, and all powerful, and because of that God can control and manage what He does not determine—i.e. He is sovereign. He can do what He pleases (Psalms 115:3, 135:6)! "All His actions are consistent with the nature of His being, a fact which is essential to His integrity and which does not in any way impinge on His sovereignty."[36] Furthermore, He has graciously revealed His nature and attributes to us in Scripture. To say that He cannot make a sovereign choice to determine faith by libertarian freedom, (not Calvinistic compatibilism) the condition of receiving salvation actually removes His sovereignty, replaces it with a human view, and confines God to man's limited understanding. As A.W. Tozer has insightfully said:

God sovereignly decreed that man should be free to exercise moral choice, and man from the beginning has fulfilled that decree by making his choice between good and evil. When he chooses to do evil, he does not thereby countervail the sovereign will of God but fulfills it, inasmuch as the eternal decree decided not which choice the man should make but that he should be free to make it. If in His absolute freedom God has willed to give man limited freedom, who is there to stay His hand or say, 'What doest thou?' Man's will is free because God is sovereign. A God less than sovereign could not bestow moral freedom upon His creatures. He would be afraid to do so.[37]

A few verses should be sufficient to make the case against irresistible grace. Stephen, in Acts 7:51, said to the Jewish Religious Council: "Ye stiffnecked and uncircumcised in heart and ears, ye do always resist the Holy Ghost: as your fathers did, so do ye." It seems that man can certainly "resist" God the Holy Spirit. It would be silly to argue that the Jewish leadership had historically resisted God's attempts to convince them to believe, when God was the one making them do it. The point is not that they just *resisted* God, but they resisted God's efforts to bring them to faith. It is an absurdity to claim that God did not secretly give them an "effectual call" while at the same time sending prophets and His word to draw them to faith, especially, when faith is the very thing God was trying to accomplish in their lives! In 2 Chronicles 36:15-16 it says, "The LORD God of their ancestors continually warned them through his messengers, for he felt compassion for his people and his dwelling place. But they mocked God's messengers, despised his warnings, and ridiculed his prophets. Finally the LORD got very angry at his people and there was no one who could prevent his judgment" (NET). Stephen referred in his rebuke of the Jewish leaders to this kind of historical resistance against God. Does this honestly sound like God is the one determining the Jews to mock His messengers, despise His warnings and ridicule His prophets? Moreover, does it make sense that God would be angry with people who are only doing what He determined them to do? Also, let us not overlook that Stephen says "Ye stiffnecked....ye do always resist...so do ye." Was Stephen confused? Of course not! For Isaiah makes this clear when he asks, "Who hath believed our report? and to whom is the arm of the LORD revealed" (Isaiah 53:1)? The apostle John strengthens that clarity when he quotes Isaiah 53:1 in his description of the Jewish leadership rejecting Jesus: "Though he had done so many miracles before them, yet they believed not on him: That the saying of Esaias the prophet might be fulfilled, which he spake, Lord, who hath believed our report? and to whom hath the arm of the Lord been revealed" (John 12:37-38)? Certainly, to say that Jesus did the miracles to convince them, but God did not want them to be convinced, destroys the sense of the passage and puts Jesus at odds with the Father. We know this cannot be true for Jesus said, "I do always those things that please him [God the Father]" (John 8:29). Additionally, Paul said in Acts 13:46 to the Jews who rejected the gospel, "It was necessary that the word of God should first have been spoken to you: but seeing ye put it from you, and judge yourselves unworthy of everlasting life, lo, we turn to the Gentiles." Later in Acts 28:28, after a different group of Jews rejected the gospel Paul said, "Be it known therefore unto you, that the salvation of God is sent unto the Gentiles, and that they will hear it." It is abundantly clear from these few verses that people can resist "the grace of God that bringeth salvation [and] hath appeared to all men" (Titus 2:11).

A simple search in the Bible for "stiff-necked" or "would not hearken" yields very interesting results. Zechariah in rebuke of Israel said, "But they refused to hearken, and pulled away the shoulder, and stopped their ears, that they should not hear. Yea, they made their hearts as an adamant stone, lest they should hear the law, and the words which the LORD of hosts hath sent in his spirit by the former prophets: therefore came a great wrath from the LORD of hosts" (Zech. 7:11-12). Therefore, no matter what God did, Israel resisted Him. Their history can be summed up in Psalm 81:11: "But my people would not hearken to my voice; and Israel would none of me." It is abundantly clear from Scripture man can resist God. To claim otherwise changes His word, dishonors His character, and distorts the image of God in man.

RESPONSE TO PERSEVERANCE OF THE SAINTS

Our last point in the 5-Point T.U.L.I.P. acronym focuses on the ability of the elect to persevere until the end. The logic is simple: since God unconditionally elects (U) those who He wants to save, because they are dead (T) and unable to respond to the gospel, He then atones for them through Christ (L), regenerates them (I) and finally makes sure that they remain in faith until the end of their life (P). In other words, they persevere and God makes sure they will *not* fall away.

I would like to make two comments regarding this before any analysis. First, this is a good place to understand what people normally tend to grasp regarding Calvinism because most naive enthusiasts focus on this particular point before the other four. They think Calvinism is a theology that teaches a person cannot lose your salvation, hence the perseverance aspect. Therefore, if they want to believe in eternal security (though this can be understood in varying nuances and not Calvinistic teachings only), they choose Calvinism as opposed to Arminianism because Arminians tend to believe (though not all do) that a person can commit apostasy and end up eternally lost. This is an unfortunate shallow view of the Calvinistic (and Arminian) systems since those who do not understand Calvinism are latching on to it based on the final point which, when properly understood, does not present the security many are looking for (explanation to follow). Second, at this point in the T.U.L.I.P. line of thinking, people cannot truly be Calvinists if they start to eliminate Points, which many tend to do. For one reason or another, many consider themselves 4, 3 or even 2-Point Calvinists, which means they are really not Calvinists at all. The system stands or falls based on accepting the Points properly understood, not simply picking and choosing the ones that appeal. If you want to be a true Calvinist, opposed to some hybrid of your own making, you need to accept the 5 Points. That is Calvinism! It would be both silly and naive to say, "I do not believe in the first four points of Calvinism, but I like the fifth point because I believe in eternal security; so I'm a Calvinist," because Calvinism does not equal one point or two or three, etc. Calvinism is the entire system which is how it works. Many Calvinists have varying nuances within their adherence to the 5 Points, but they essentially believe them. I think the only significant distinction is between what I call consistent Calvinists (who believe like Calvin) and the inconsistent Calvinists (who adopt compatibilism). But, both groups at least maintain the 5 Points and do not adjust the theology to personal tastes.

Some Calvinists tend to shy away from limited atonement or irresistible grace because the points seem unbiblical, yet attempt to keep the rest of the system. However, breaking up the system removes the system's logic that connects each doctrinal link. Again, at that point, it is not Calvinism anymore because it really does not correlate to John Calvin's theology, nor will the Points make any sense theologically (within the Calvinistic definitions). As mentioned, the system is a logical flow of one Point built upon another; each cog makes the wheel turn. This is one reason why I have taken the space to examine the 5 Points and the Calvinistic definitions for a proper understanding of the system. It is easy to argue against a strawman, but I want to avoid that and make sure we are discussing the actual problems with the Points as Calvinists understand them.

Moving on, a short analysis should suffice for easy rebuttal of the problems with this last Point. I would like to mention that in my analysis of this Point, I am not making a case against a Christian holding to eternal security. Calvinism notwithstanding, many evangelicals believe in eternal security for various reasons and with various nuances. Some do not believe that a Christian can commit apostasy, while other evangelicals hold to a form of eternal security, yet do believe there are conditions of apostasy. Nevertheless, I am not discussing evangelical aspects of eternal security; I am focusing on the last Point in the T.U.L.I.P. acronym and how it has biblical problems as it relates to its Calvinistic definition.

To put it simply, the perseverance of the saints teaches that a person only knows they are elect if they endure until the end of their life. The obvious question is, what does Calvin mean by persevere? In other words, how do the "elect" know that they are persevering (i.e. that they are the "elect"), if they struggle with sin or have other areas of difficulty in life that call their faith into question at certain points (no pun intended)? All Christians are subject to some form of struggle with sin, but the "elect" should maintain good works to demonstrate their persevering condition. This requires some standard of measurement, but no one Calvinist seems to be able to define that unquestioned criteria. Calvinists have put forth varying assessments of good works and perseverance over the years, but this is not a solution. It is only a perspective to provide one person's convictions to evaluate something that only God can know (2 Tim. 2:19). Thus, the two problems that plague this Point is first to know if a person is persevering and thereby has the assurance he or she is elect, and second, the knowledge of what the standard measurement is to evaluate whether perseverance is genuine or not. The problem is, these two issues end up playing off each other with a confusing result. For example, I think I am elect because I am doing well in my good works and consider this evidence of my perseverance. However, if I fall into sin, does that mean that I am not elect? How shall I know? What sin or measure of sin is acceptable before I am a false believer? Who makes that decision? Who evaluates me: someone else or do I judge my own condition? What if I struggle with a particular sin but am for the most part having victory; does that remove me from the elect list or am I still persevering? Moreover, what if I am doing well in good works am I trusting them for my salvation? I am encouraged to focus on good works; however, is there too much focus? To be sure, these questions can plague non-Calvinists, but the Calvinistic system unintentionally breeds these kinds of struggles by the nature of its design. Reading a few Calvinistic blogs can easily make the case for this aspect of the problem. This attempt to establish a standard and thereby define the good works of the elect can result in the opposite effect in many believers' lives. Instead of encouraging them that they are the "elect," it can pit them against a list of standards that, if not kept, result in condemnation and the fear that they may not be "elect." This is a rarely discussed side of the problems inherent within Calvinism. This is a concern for many within Calvinistic circles, since it hits exactly where everyone lives. Believers are in different areas of spiritual development, and having a subjective measurement to determine if they are "elect" is anything but helpful. Unfortunately, various preachers and leaders within the Reformed tradition (with some disagreement) try to establish an objective measurement. Even though the Bible is used to create the criteria, it is the nature of the Calvinistic system that increases the burden of performance on the believers. This is where the doctrinal positions create the operational problems. What we believe will eventually find its way to our behavior.

Since many Calvinistic proponents do not believe the Bible teaches that a regenerated believer has a sin nature, this compounds the problem for living the Christian life. Either a believer is in constant sanctifying development or they are most likely not one of the "elect." The idea of a carnal believer is unacceptable within this theological framework, though Paul was the one that spoke about carnality as a real problem among believers (1 Cor. 3:1-3). Paul divided the world into the saved and the unsaved. The unsaved he called "natural" (1 Cor. 2:14), meaning that they live by their natural senses since they have no spiritual life to sense the things of the Holy Spirit. Among the saved, he divided them up into 3 categories; babes, carnal, and spiritual (i.e. spiritually mature). Brand new babes in Christ are a thrill to see and encouragement to any congregation, but they need to be watched carefully just like little babies. Babies are cute to watch, but they need constant supervision because everything they can get their hands on goes right into their mouth. This can be dangerous, unhealthy, and in extreme cases, can cause death. Babes in Christ are no different. Whatever they "hear" is taken in as the gospel truth. With their newfound faith and an open heart to God, they have an openness that was not there previously. They tend to think that anything a Christian says is true—especially if they are on TV or in a Christian book. Their openness is natural and exciting, but they must be careful or they can consume things that will derail their Christian experience and cause them great harm. This being the case with almost every new believer, it is a critical time in their development and recognizing they still have a sin nature is essential. To assign their potential sinful struggles to a history of habit in their old life disarms them in the real spiritual battle they face and the potential of their existing sin nature. The point here is that Calvinism creates an idealistic Christian experience ahead of time based on their theology, not on the Bible. The perseverance aspect can easily change from the normal Christian endurance against sin to a legalistic formula of Christian living to maintain elect status. By the time you reach the fifth Point, the entire focus is on good works, so the focus then returns to Point two so the Calvinist can be secure in their election. For some it goes on and on bouncing back and forth between the two Points to gain a measure of security. Not an enviable Christian experience to say the least. But this is the problem when theological systems replace the simple teaching of God's word. I know, I lived there for a few years; it's not pleasant.

Spiritual believers are more aware regarding the dangers of taking all Christian teaching and books as true; they are typically on guard for biblical error. They have had their senses developed by a working knowledge of the Bible (Heb. 5:14); this applies to Calvinists or non-Calvinists. But in the Calvinistic world, how are the carnal believers managed, or do they even exist in Christianity? They do according to Paul, and within every Christian church, they definitely exist—to the chagrin of many Calvinists. Life would be wonderful if carnality did not exist, but it is a fact that will remain with us until "the redemption of our bodies" (Rom. 8:20). A Christian stunted in their spiritual development is more often than not a carnal Christian. When Christians should be maturing in their faith but become stagnant, they become carnal, i.e. "dull of hearing" and unable to eat food that is for mature believers. Tragically, they still need to be bottle fed (1 Cor. 3:1-2; Heb. 5:11-13). Unfortunately, in some churches that reject the notion of a carnal believer, a truly carnal Christian cannot eat the diet of the more mature believers and they starve due to a lack of milk feeding, which can compound their condition. They either will often fall away or end up moving to a church that will be patient with them and nurture them to good spiritual health. I have seen it happen repeatedly over the more than 30 years I have been a pastor. But don't misunderstand me, I'm not saying everyone who looks like a carnal believer *is* a carnal believer because carnal believers look so much like the natural (unsaved) man. It is difficult at times to know. It definitely requires discernment and care; we should not use a broad brush to treat all who appear carnal as if unsaved. As Paul said, he had to teach them as if they were babes, though they should have matured beyond that stage (1 Cor. 3:1-3). Therefore, patience and discernment are necessary; carnality in Christians' lives can be both frustrating and time-consuming for pastors. I know this by experience.

To mischaracterize a carnal Christian as an unbeliever can do irreparable damage to their growth in Christ. Every congregation that is teaching the Bible will have all three; babes, carnal and spiritual. The mature are bringing people to Christ resulting in babes, and not all grow at the same rate or develop to the same levels of maturity, which at times results in carnality. As I mentioned, the carnal believer can cause much angst to those burdened with caring for them and trying to bring them to spiritual maturity. A way to discover whether a Christian is carnal or spiritual may be observed in their life application; the carnal believers are self-centered, where spiritual believers are Christ-centered. The self-centered perspectives cause the carnal Christian to look, and at times act, like the "natural man" who is unsaved, and this is where the problems lie. Within Calvinism, this throws a monkey wrench into the machinery of their system because you cannot have an "elect" believer appear to be living carnally. This would mean (in their theology) God has determined the stunted growth and this is only the beginning of the challenge. With all the mess and difficulty resulting from carnality, the simple solution is to eliminate carnality as a category among believers and move from babe to spiritual. This is a nice fantasy to entertain, but any cursory reading of the NT reveals that churches faced problems and needed correction. At times, that correction was against carnality, as in Paul's first letter to the Corinthians. He defines the problem in the first three chapters of the epistle.

To compound this problem, the lordship salvation teaching has tried to eliminate carnality altogether in Christianity, not just among the Reformed. This is a favorite of some Calvinists in combating the idea of a carnal believer and making it too easy to be saved, or what they call "easy believism." I am sure they feel it kills two birds with one stone; unfortunately, it is not a biblical stone. Lordship salvation teaches that a person must understand exactly what it means for Jesus to be the Lord over all of their lives and somehow demonstrate a willingness to repent—more than just express it. In lordship salvation, simply believing the gospel and exercising faith in Christ falls short of salvation—there is not enough teeth in simple belief for these folks. Now, what I am not saying is that simply mouthing words is adequate for a person to be saved. If we share the gospel with someone that desires Christ, we need to receive them for God does—if they are genuine. But only God knows if their belief is genuine or not; we can only take them at their word and observe their lives. There will always be make-believers, but we cannot change the gospel to eliminate or triage them. Coming up with unbiblical teachings that add to the gospel message simply to adhere to a Reformed system of soteriology is at a minimum enormously problematic. At certain points, it can be heresy if there is any added condition to simple faith in Christ (see Paul's Galatian letter).

No one in Christian leadership is happy with the carnality seen in the church today. It is the source of many church splits and various disruptions within churches on a regular basis. However, in trying to define it out of existence by swinging the doctrinal pendulum to the opposite extreme, not only does not address the problem, but also simply pushes it into a more problematic category. Lordship salvation conflates the doctrine of salvation and sanctification together and this results in classic legalism. It is adding to the gospel, and frankly, it is heretical. When you begin to add to the gospel any requirements beyond faith, even things that belong to the doctrine of sanctification, you have entered into Galatianism. This is the very thing that Paul warned against in his letter to the Galatians. Lordship salvation is the error of solving a problem with a heresy that results in begetting a second heresy, and these result in doctrinal dominoes falling until believers are confused and condemned. The tragic consequence of this teaching is exactly what it tries to avoid—apostasy! Lordship salvation front-loads the gospel so heavily with sanctification requirements to avoid any carnality and future apostasy that it actually creates it.

Many who think they are "elect" that might fall into carnality for a time may give up and call it quits thinking they were never one of the "elect" to begin with. On the other hand, to avoid apostasy and keep up appearances, carnality becomes masked in legalistic and self-righteous behavior which is equally destructive (remember the Pharisees?). For many struggling believers, it is easier for them to leave the church than stay and feel like a pretender. Honest people realize that they are struggling with their sin nature and some realize their own carnality. But the rigid requirements of Calvinistic Lordship salvation is not the solution; it can be just as much a problem as carnality. It has been well said, when a Christian's spiritual life deteriorates, they either backslide into sin (carnality), or front slide into legalism. Christians should avoid both of these roads at all costs.

An illustration may help bring this problem to light. Living in the Boston area, for years we have had to deal with the Boston Church of Christ (BCOC). While working in Boston in the 80's and some of the 90's, I would frequently see BCOC disciples on the trains and at times converse with them. They are an offshoot of the Church of Christ denomination, but extreme in their views and cultic in their mind control practices.[38] I have met a number of people who were victims of their controlling practices and received calls from families asking if we had cult recovery operations to save their children from the BCOC. Once they get their tentacles on you, it is very difficult—and at times impossible—to recover college age kids or young people (BCOC's main target) from their powerful psychological indoctrination. They center much of their doctrinal positions on Acts 2:38, and claim that to become a Christian, baptism in water is required (baptismal regeneration); additionally, the baptism must be performed by them. But before they will agree to baptize a potential convert, they require them to live like a Christian in various ways to demonstrate their dedication and commitment. Only after their allegiance is confirmed by loyal living, can they be baptized into the BCOC and become one of the "true" last day's remnant church. This is not only a doctrinal disaster considering the baptismal regeneration, but also a legalistic prison from day one. If a person can live the Christian life unconverted, what is that saying? It tells the BCOC potential convert that keeping outward practices is what Christianity is since they are required to observe commandments and live like a NT disciple prior to their "salvation." Theoretically, after they are saved (baptized), the only thing that changes is that they get wet in the baptismal tank and receive membership in the BCOC. This method is too close (to the lordship salvation method of bringing sanctification practices into the salvation process) for comfort. The BCOC is a cult and a dangerous one at that. But what can be equally dangerous is lordship salvation, because it is touted by respected Christian leaders and the unsuspecting victims of its burdened gospel are vulnerable Christians. Unbelievers will typically shy away from such frontloaded gospel requirements which leaves carnal or weak Christians who will adhere to the legalistic requirements of this teaching, only to fall into further legalism assuming that this is normal NT Christianity. They then create their own lordship disciples etc. etc. If you have an improperly calibrated GPS, the further you travel towards your expected destination, the further off course you will go. If you start out with doctrinal error at salvation, the further you go into sanctification the further off you will go; there is no way to avoid it. No matter what the problems are in the church and with Christians in general, the gospel of Jesus Christ is not to be touched or adjusted. Paul gives the most dire warning to those who do (Gal. 1:8-9).

A final note is warranted regarding the Calvinistic teaching on perseverance. Though Calvin disagreed with the Council of Trent (AD 1547) on the addition of works contributing to justification, he did not entirely break from it. When his view of perseverance is properly understood, it never actually provides security to the believer, as most evangelicals today understand eternal security. For the Calvinist, they never actually know if they are eternally secure until the end--it's the system! Calvin admittedly embraced Augustine's theology wholeheartedly.[39] Augustine believed that a person could possess genuine faith and appear to be elect, but fall away, never actually having been one of the elect. "Augustine said the non-elect can have genuine faith. Augustine said the non-elect can be legitimately regenerated by the Holy Spirit. But because they have not received that most necessary of all gifts, the gift of perseverance, these regenerated believers are non-elect."[40] Aside from the troubling theology of Augustine, it was Calvin's adherence to this concept that creates the real difficulty:

> I know that to attribute faith to the reprobate seems hard to some, when Paul declares it is the result of election. Yet this difficulty is easily solved. For though only those predestined to salvation receive the light of faith and truly feel the power of the gospel, yet experience shows that the reprobate are sometimes affected by almost the same feeling as the elect, so that even in their own judgment they do not in any way differ from the elect. Therefore it is not at all absurd that the apostle should attribute to them a taste of the heavenly gift and -- Christ, faith for a time; not because they firmly grasp the force of spiritual grace and the sure light of faith, but because the Lord, to render them more convicted and inexcusable, steals into their minds to the extent that his goodness may be tasted without the Spirit of adoption.[41]

Therefore, a person could appear elect, have what Calvin called "temporary faith," and still end up in hell. What drives this kind of confusing theology? Certainly not the Bible as normally read and understood. Please note, Calvin bases his theology on what "experience shows", not what the Bible teaches. Moreover, this is his perspective on what he observes. The point here (again, no pun intended) is that to maintain a warped theology, it is necessary that unbiblical theological manipulations must be created to explain away what the Bible makes clear. Calvin's view on perseverance only compounds the difficulty for a disciple of his when they attempt to gain some assurance of their salvation prior to the end. Yet the Bible is in direct conflict with this view. John said, "Beloved, now are we the sons of God" (1 John 3:1), and "These things I have written to you who believe in the name of the Son of God, that you may know that you have eternal life" (1 John 5:13). Thus, John says, "*now* are we the sons of God", which can only mean that people are assured of their salvation, else, how can John say *now*? In addition, he wrote so that those who do believe may know that they "have eternal life;" thus it is by belief, not works. How can they know if their evaluation is based on Calvinism? Maybe they only have "temporary faith." How is this simple teaching by the apostle overlooked by Calvin and Calvinists? I believe it is because they view the Bible through Calvinism, instead of judging Calvinism by the Bible.

This theology inspires biblical confusion and a removal of the assurance of salvation that so many unaware Christians believe what this Point on perseverance teaches. So when properly understood within the T.U.L.I.P. system and Calvin's own teachings, this fifth Point steals the assurance of salvation and prevents a believer from ever truly knowing if they are elect--even if they have faith and their faith is accompanied by good works. Is it any wonder why there is such stress and anxiety among Calvinists? If they are one of the elect, they will not know that until the end; if they are not one of the elect but only seem to be, they will not find that out until the end either. This theology unnecessarily overburdens believers and creates what it ostensibly tries to remove, a lack of assurance of salvation. Though Calvin disagreed with The Council of Trent on the addition of works in justification, he developed a theology that was in the sense worse, since believers are motivated to do works so they can assure themselves that they are elect. But because of the nature of never truly knowing until the end, even among those who seem to be doing well in their faith, they can still end up in hell. Calvin seemed to end up back to where he started when part of the Roman Catholic Church, combining justification and sanctification and adding works as a means of security. Calvin's theology has its roots in Augustine, Roman Catholicism, and his own unbiblical development. Thus, believers should know exactly what they are signing up for when they decide to be Calvin's disciple. Theologically, the Twilight Zone has nothing on Calvin.

REDISCOVERING HISTORY

If we have learned anything from history, it is that those who do not learn from it are destined to repeat it—in the negative sense anyway, which is the problem. This is one of the issues when it comes to the doctrine of John Calvin. His views actually began with Augustine, the bishop of Hippo back in the 4th century. But before mentioning some problematic conclusions Augustine arrived at, it should be recognized that he was a brilliant man and insightful philosopher. He possessed, as his writings attest, a powerfully persuasive intellectual ability. We have received by way of his philosophical and ethical writings very helpful arguments for God's existence and the Christian faith. He was honest in the written expressions of the nature of sin and its power through temptation. His work in defense of the Christian faith is both commendable and in many aspects, successful—we still borrow some of his arguments. However, in attempts to bring about a successful defeat of his rivals, I believe he swung the pendulum too far in the opposite direction, a problem repeated by many today. Winning an argument is admirable when done with intellectual skill and well organized points, but winning does not assure the correctness of the points, for many times the truth does not prevail. The more skillful debater, not necessarily those standing on the side of truth, is the winner of many debates. When those with an accurate knowledge of the truth possess this type of debating skill, productive educational results typically follow. But when people cling to the debater through personal admiration because of the "win," the man himself becomes the object of loyalty instead of his solid conclusive arguments presented. Hero worship is not uncommon; even Paul the apostle had to confront it (1 Cor. 1:12, 3:4). When a generation possesses a powerful intellect like Augustine, it is easy for him to influence those appreciative of his leadership, especially when it comes to his defense of the Christian faith. Who does not appreciate the leaders in our own time among those who champion the cause of Christ in the marketplace of ideas, especially those who have suffered unjustly because of it?

In Augustine's case, he changed his views on particular aspects of Christian theology which resulted in his philosophical conclusions when debating those he disagreed with. One has to wonder if those he debated motivated the progressive changes in his theology. Did he find it easier to defeat opposing positions by adjusting his theology, or was it adjusted personally and that created the opposition to whom he debated? This is up for debate (no pun intended). But regarding our present subject of Augustine's theological change, a highly recommended and thorough work on the subject is available by Dr. Ken Wilson, called *The Foundation Of Augustinian–Calvinism*.[42] Dr. Wilson actually read all the writings of Augustine sequentially as he wrote them and represents his (Augustine's) beliefs in his book. The following is a very brief analysis of Augustine's history of theological change related to our present subject.

Augustine was a Manichaean Gnostic for nine years prior to converting to Christianity. Manichaean Gnostics and Stoics were determinative in their beliefs, which means they did not believe in free will and held to a fatalistic worldview. The easiest way to think of determinism is that all things are predetermined and therefore it is fruitless to attempt to change things. This is fatalism, a philosophy that is dead-ended because there is nothing that can change the future, so why try? Those who follow horoscopes (which I do not recommend) believe this type of fatalism. The average adherent to horoscopes will read them in the morning prior to leaving their home. If the horoscope tells them it will be a bad day, they may call into work sick and stay home. They believe staying home will help them avoid the negative consequences of the horoscope prediction for that day. What they fail to understand is that whether they stay home or go to work, the horoscope has told them it will be a bad day, and that bad day will not change based on their location. So in the end, they've used a sick day unnecessarily, lied to their boss, lived in fear all day, and may run out of sick days before the end of their work year if the horoscopes do not paint a fair picture of some of the days ahead. This in essence is the application of a deterministic, fatalistic philosophy. It disconnects a person from reality and is therefore a fruitless, valueless, logically inconsistent path in life. From a Christian perspective, it is idolatry and an immorality to be avoided at God's command (Deut. 18:10; Isaiah 8:19-20, 47:11-15; Daniel 2:2-10; Gal. 5:20).

The initial deterministic influence on Augustine was Stoicism, which taught every minute event in the universe is controlled by fate. The Stoic philosopher Lucius Annaeus Seneca said, "Fate leads the willing and drags along the unwilling."[43] This certainly is a fatalistic representation of their belief. Fate is understood as a power that has the capability to order the course of events in history. We see this concept popularized in many Hollywood movies where the actors talk about "fate" bringing them together. Obviously there is no decision-making capability in a mindless force to which we attribute some aspect of intellectual capability. Also brought out in movies is the belief that the "universe" has some particular destiny-producing capability. The actors express how because they followed their "hearts," the universe is happy with them or they sense a harmony with it. This is also a nonsensical perspective since only a being that possesses personhood can make thoughtful decisions. On a scale beyond the universe, which is required to control the events within the universe, there must be a Being that has the capability to control future events, the power to control them, the intelligence to design their outcome, a purpose for why, and will to decide to do them in the first place. Nonetheless, people tend to believe that mindless energies and sometimes the stars in the sky guide and direct them in their future events and fated destinies. This may make for a decent storyline in a movie; however, when it comes to reality it is no more worthy of trust than waiting for Superman to save us from Lex Luthor. It is a fantasy better left to entertainment on the big screen, not a foundational basis for real life.

Augustine eventually embraced Manichaean Gnosticism which was dualistic in its philosophical view of the universe; in dualism, everything made of matter is evil and the spiritual or non-material is good. Additionally, Manichaean Gnosticism was equal in determinism as Stoicism. "Augustine of Hippo adhered to the Manichaean faith for nine years before his Christian conversion...he felt exempted from any responsibility for his own sin due to the Manichaean fatalism."[44] Note the natural application of this philosophy; exemption from personal responsibility. Determinism is attractive because no matter what a person does, they attribute the responsibility to the determinative powers that control them and their history. This is one of the problems with pagan beliefs and the resulting application of their beliefs in daily living. This philosophy had a definite influence on Augustine. However, after his initial conversion to Christianity, he started out *against* the deterministic fatalism of his Manichaean background. It was not until Augustine opposed the claims of Pelagius, a monk and his contemporary that he began to change. Pelagius taught that man had the ability to be sinless apart from the supernatural grace of God, and combating this free will position led Augustine back into his deterministic framework. "During and after the Pelagian controversy, Augustine developed a doctrine of predestination in accordance with his doctrine of unmerited "operating grace." God chooses the elect gratuitously, without any previous merit on their part, and even before the foundation of the world God predestines who the elect are."[45] This decision of God to predestine some to eternal life and others to eternal death without any apparent reason would become the foundation for John Calvin's theology.

John Calvin took Augustine's theological determinism and not only repeated it, but developed and refined it further. Calvin himself said, "Augustine is so wholly with me, that if I wished to write a confession of my faith, I could do so with all fulness and satisfaction to myself out of his writings. ...And it would be more manifest still, could the whole line of his confession be adduced, how fully and solidly he agrees with me in every particular."[46] This John Calvin effectively did, which is reflected in the systematic theology he wrote when he was 27 years old, called "Institutes of the Christian Religion." Calvin made it clear that in his view, man has no free will, but God determines all from eternity. He said, "We call predestination God's eternal decree, by which he compacted with himself what he willed to become of each man. For all are not created in equal condition; rather, eternal life is foreordained for some, eternal damnation for others. Therefore, as any man has been created for one or the other of these ends, we speak of him to life or to death."[47] Further, Calvin said:

> As Scripture, then, clearly shows, we say that God once established by his eternal and unchangeable plan those whom he long before determined once for all to receive into salvation, and those whom, on the other hand, he would devote to destruction. We assert that, with respect to the elect, this plan was founded on His freely given mercy, without regard to human worth; but by his just and irreprehensible but incomprehensible judgment he has barred the door of life to those whom he has given over to damnation.[48]

This doctrine is called double predestination or the doctrine of reprobation. Additionally, referring to Romans 9:13 ("As it is written, Jacob have I loved, but Esau have I hated"), Calvin said:

> ...the reprobate are raised up to the end that through them God's glory may be revealed. Finally, he [Paul] adds the conclusion that "God has mercy on whomever he wills". Do you see how Paul attributes both to God's decision alone? If, then, we cannot determine a reason why he vouchsafes mercy to his own, except that it so pleases him, neither shall we have any reason for rejecting others, other than his will. For when it is said that God hardens or shows mercy to whom he wills, men are warned to seek no cause outside his will.[49]

Calvin's commentary on the Bible reflects his deterministic views, but he vacillates at times. His perspectives on eternal predestination is in contradiction to some of his own statements. When commenting on 2 Peter 3:9, which states, "The Lord is not slack concerning his promise, as some men count slackness; but is longsuffering to us-ward, not willing that any should perish, but that all should come to repentance," he says:

> So wonderful is his love towards mankind, that he would have them all to be saved ... that God is ready to receive all to repentance, so that none may perish; for in these words the way and manner of obtaining salvation is pointed out. ...But it may be asked, If God wishes none to perish, why is it that so many do perish? To this my answer is, that no mention is here made of the hidden purpose of God, according to which the reprobate are doomed to their own ruin, but only of his will as made known to us in the gospel. For God there stretches forth his hand without a difference to all, but lays hold only of those, to lead them to himself, whom he has chosen before the foundation of the world.[50]
> (Calvin's Commentary on 2 Peter 3:9)

Could it be he appears to contradict his own position when working through these Scriptures because the Bible is at variance to his theology? This logical contradiction between what the Scripture says and what Calvin says is clearly a problem. He states that through the gospel we know God's will, that God stretches His hand out to all. This is true and the statement on its own is acceptable because it essentially restates what the Scripture teaches. Unfortunately, Calvin does not seem to believe what he plainly states. He mentions that there is a "hidden purpose of God" that is not mentioned in 1 Peter 3:9. In the passage, Calvin understands that even though Peter does not tell us there is a secret work of God to elect some and damn others, it is there nonetheless. Calvin deliberately changed what the verse plainly says, which is not reflective of integrity to the text. He logically contradicts himself by violating the text, which is a strong accusation, but the evidence of self-contradiction is there. The problem of logical contradictions related to theology receives attention in the chapter entitled Rediscovering Logic. There we observe how to think, which is rooted in how God created man in His image.

REDISCOVERING CONTEXT

Remembering context can be a constant struggle for Bible students. Chapters and verses can work in our favor or trip us up. The chapter breaks are very helpful for searching and locating verses for varying subjects, but this advantage can easily become a disadvantage. When Paul wrote Romans, it was a letter without chapters or verses. The change in subject is evident to the reader, since there is a normal transition to the next subject for a logical reason. Though Romans chapter 8 is not the subject of our focus, it is nonetheless important to know what Paul teaches there so the transition to Romans 9 will not lose connection with his flow of thought from chapter 8.

Paul completes his teaching on the sanctification of the believer in the first half of Romans 8 and the second half of the chapter transitions to the glorification of the believer. A careful reading of Romans 8 reveals the apostle is trying to encourage those who are suffering because in distressing situations comfort does not always translate into what we perceive as God's best in life for Christians. Therefore, Paul attempts to encourage the Romans because of the pain and suffering they were facing. In verses 16 and 17 he says, "The Spirit itself beareth witness with our spirit, that we are the children of God: And if children, then heirs; heirs of God, and joint-heirs with Christ; if so be that we suffer with him, that we may be also glorified together." In these verses, Paul transitions from the sanctifying work of the Spirit of God to the future glory promised to those in Christ. Paul explains that in this present life while being sanctified, believers have the "Spirit of adoption" because of the presence of the Holy Spirit in the believer, as he says in verse 15. The Spirit's presence creates a yearning for the completed work of redemption and the realization of the full adoption—which is "the redemption of our body" (v. 23). It is in glory that believers actually receive the full inheritance promised. Paul then provides the evidence—as he typically does—of that promised work of God in the verses that follow verse 23.

The verses in Romans 8:28-39 are the demonstration of God's faithfulness to bring believers to glory, despite the challenging circumstances they face that constantly assail their faith while in this present world. Verses 28-30 are variously interpreted depending upon theological perspective. Some understand that in these verses God speaks of believers in the past tense, that He sees the work as already completed, i.e. "glorified" as in verse 30. It would have to be the past tense according to this view since the ones Paul wrote to had not yet been "glorified," and that word ends the string of words describing believers ("foreknew...predestinate...called...justified...glorified"). This is a common view among evangelicals. There are other views, but the nuances will not affect the interpretation enough to change the transition from chapter 8 to 9.

The point of this passage is the assurance all believers have that God *will* bring them to glory, regardless of the circumstances in their lives that cry out contrary to that. Christians should keep circumstances in perspective and never allow them to overrule God's faithfulness. Suffering can easily distort our view of God and His promises, but as Paul says, nothing can separate believers from His love (8:35-39). Nor should believers see adverse circumstances as a measurement to evaluate God's love. Paul made it clear earlier in Romans that God's love was demonstrated through the work of the cross (Rom. 5), and this is the criteria that believers are to use. Circumstances and the emotions that surround them constantly fluctuate, but the love of God to all was demonstrated publicly on Calvary as the Son of God gave His life for the world —this will never change!

As has been said, Romans 8 begins with "no condemnation" and ends with "no separation." Having established God's faithfulness to the Roman believers, Paul now moves into Romans 9 to teach a crucial and sensitive topic—that of Israel in their current state of the rejection of Jesus of Nazareth as their Messiah. It might be asked, and assuredly Paul had this in mind when he penned the letter, how can these Roman believers trust that God will work everything out to their "good" (Rom. 8:28) when the nation God created to bring the gospel in the first place is not currently in good standing with Him? As is his manner, Paul anticipates the question and fully answers this crucial issue regarding the nation of Israel in Romans chapters 9 through 11. He eventually gets to the application section of the letter in Romans 12, where he will "beseech" them to "present" themselves to God as a "living sacrifice," grounded in all that he previously taught. But how can they do this with the elephant in the room—that of Israel's present situation? Did not Israel offer themselves to God and eventually end up in this place of unbelief and rejection? Could the Roman believers end up in the same situation—could we? Did not God make promises to the nation of Israel? Why are they in a situation that appears contrary to all the OT promises God made through Abraham, Isaac, and Jacob? These are the questions Paul must put to rest so the state of the nation of Israel can be removed as a stumbling block for the Roman believers at that time, and current believers today. Romans 8 helps prepare us for the context of these chapters. Therefore, in these chapters Paul tells us why Israel is in their present state of rejection and what will happen to them in the future. Indeed, Paul solves the dilemma of the nation for Christians and for Jews.

Why is the context so important in this epistle, or any epistle for that matter? The answer should be obvious. Without knowing the context, the natural thing to do would be to add a context. How could Paul's letter or any other writing for that matter be understood if it lacked context? It couldn't! So how do we discover the context of a biblical writing? There are principles that when properly observed, help us discover the author's context to more accurately understand the author's words. Many of these principles, as we will see, are self-evident once understood. In the discipline of hermeneutics, context is a critical rule which we will examine next.

REDISCOVERING HERMENEUTICS

Before we enter the exposition of Romans 9, we need to understand biblical hermeneutics. Hermeneutics is the science of Bible interpretation, or the principles used to interpret the Bible. It is a developed method of study to understand the Bible within the framework of when, how, why, and by whom it was written. When we read the Bible, as with any book, the writer has something they wish to communicate. The Bible is the same as other books in that it has a message to communicate; the difference being it is God's inspired word (lit. "God-breathed," 2 Tim. 3:16). Inspiration does not mean that the educational level, intellectual capacity, or emotional condition of the writer is changed or bypassed. God uses each of the writer's natural capabilities but brings about an inerrant and infallible writing. God spoke through the OT and NT writers to provide us His word in a clear and understandable framework. Certainly, as with this book or any book, effort is necessary to comprehend the writing. Therefore, the Bible requires diligence in study so what the writer says is understood correctly, thereby making sense of the message. People tend to think of study in reference to difficult topics for educational or professional use, but when it comes to the Bible, they tend to treat it as a storybook or novel. This erroneous view of what the Bible is as a book has resulted in many avoiding it or mischaracterizing it. Instead of digging in to discover the truth God spoke to man, people read it as a storybook expecting it to maintain their attention as an object of entertainment such as a mystery novel would (which it

SCOTT MITCHELL

certainly can be at times), but that is not the reason for its existence. The Bible exists for a very different reason, so approaching it with a misguided expectation can shortchange the outcome. Children grow up reading the Bible as a storybook to learn the stories, but as Paul said, "When I was a child, I talked like a child, I thought like a child, I reasoned like a child. But when I became an adult, I set aside childish ways" (1 Cor. 13:11, NET). Children must transition from the storybook mentality as they grow into adolescence. Even Jesus when a "boy grew up and became strong, filled with wisdom, and God's grace was on Him" (Luke 2:40, HCSB), and it should not be any different for us. Adults need to put the effort into seeking God, and discovering what His word tells us as first priority. The Bible deserves the greatest of our care when studying it because it is not just a historical document for educational reading; it is the very words of the living God (Deut. 8:3; Matt. 4:4)! The Bible instructs us in our relationship with God, and gives hope regarding our future eternal inheritance. Secular books are limited to our temporary existence and have no value beyond this world (many don't have any temporary value either). The overriding importance of the Bible cannot be understated.

The most natural method of understanding the Bible is to read and study it within a framework that considers how it came to us. Each book in the Bible was written in a historical situation and background, so knowing the history is essential. The writer knew what he wanted to say and certainly it was understandable to him--future prophecy at times notwithstanding. Peter tells us that "prophecy came not in old time by the will of man: but holy men of God spake as they were moved by the Holy Ghost" (2 Peter 1:21). God "moved" them; literally they were "being borne along" by the Holy Spirit as they wrote. God breathed His word through them as the instruments of communicating a perfect message through imperfect people. Only God has that capability. The "inspiration" (God-breathed) relates to the written word on the page, or *graphe* ("Scripture" in 2 Tim. 3:16), so after the writer was done, the words on the page or the text as we call it, is God-breathed. Therefore, inspiration relates to the words, not the writer who is the instrument God used to pen the words. The author wrote under the inspiration of the Holy Spirit to give us God's inspired word. However, that does not mean everything the author ever wrote or said was under the inspiration of the Holy Spirit. Only the words of the Bible are inspired, which is why we focus on the text. The author is God's instrument, the product of their writing under divine inspiration is God's word.

Having said that, the historical context is essential to comprehend the text. Without it, we are lost and are left to provide our own context, which will most likely be foreign to the text. For example, if I do not know the situation that the prophet Micah spoke to, I will attempt to understand his writing in light of our 21st century context—one that would have been foreign to him. In other words, the reader will supply the context, since the original writer's context is unknown. Historical background and circumstance of writing are crucial to know the author's situational context. Therefore, we need to read the Bible in a fashion that enables us to comprehend its message as written. Once we understand it within the original context of the Scripture we are reading, then the application to our own lives becomes clearer. I must understand what the author was saying to his recipients in their context before I can understand and apply any aspect of his words to my situation.

The writers used words in sentences, so we need to know the grammar of the language in which they wrote. The OT is written in Hebrew with some minor sections of Aramaic, and the NT is written in Greek. Knowing the grammatical structure and word definitions in the original languages becomes a necessity, no different from knowing the English language with some aspect of sentence structure and word definitions so you can understand what I am writing. You do not have to be an English major to read this book, but you certainly must know enough about English to be able to read and comprehend it in its normal grammatical structure. I am an author and I have something I am trying to communicate to you; hopefully I have been somewhat successful so far. If I started putting in words you were unfamiliar with and did not supply the definitions, you would need to look them up if you wanted to know what I am saying. If I put sentences together that seemed to make no sense (hopefully that is not happening), how would you know what I was saying? You wouldn't! It is no different with the Bible. The history and grammar all need consideration so we can understand the writers.

One more point here is noteworthy. As a reader, you do not determine what I am communicating; I do. I know what I am trying to say; your job is to discover that. In other words, the reader does not determine the meaning of a writing, the writer does. The reader may miss a point or misunderstand because of the ambiguity of some statement or point, but that does not change the meaning of what was written and why. If someone read this book and said, "Mitchell is a 5 Point Calvinist," they would be entirely wrong. If that is what they concluded from what I wrote, either I was too vague, or they added their own meaning to what I wrote. Either way, I am the one that determines the meaning of my own writing, and it makes sense to me. Therefore, when reading the Bible, we cannot just make it mean what we would like it to mean or impose our own thoughts or ideas into the writer's intention. The authors of Scripture knew what they wrote and why they wrote it. It made sense to them, the Holy Spirit, and their audience at the time they wrote it. If it didn't, it cannot make any sense to anyone. Therefore, once we understand what the authors wrote in the original context, we can then see how it applies to us today.

The views I express in Romans 9 should not shock anyone (perhaps other than some Calvinists). I will exegete the passages and explain them in their own context. Using this normal hermeneutical method (literal-historical-grammatical), should flow naturally throughout the expositional section of the book. Moreover, my commentary should not be a surprise when compared to the text itself. Hopefully, it will only help clarify the text.

When examining Paul's epistles, we must be aware of his use of OT quotes. Paul (and other NT authors) quote the OT many times. When they do, its usage is related to the explanation of the OT passage within its original context since it had meaning to its original audience. If the NT writers used the OT quotes and never connected the original meaning, the quotes would not be comprehendible. Quotes are normally used to support, prove and bolster points made by authors. The NT authors connect their meaning to the OT, since the NT is fulfilling and expanding upon the OT. The Bible is a progressive revelation, which means that we have progress in truth revealed and knowledge gained over time, to a more complete understanding of revelation. Each revealed truth in the Bible builds upon, and is in harmony with, that which is previously given. There are no contradictions, only apparent ones if we limit ourselves to a cursory reading. Examining each apparent contradiction within its context, while adding a little bit of mental elbow grease, for the most part dissolves these challenges.[51] There are times NT writers quote OT passages to address a particular subject and express a point that is not a direct fulfillment of the OT passage. However, these situations are usually obvious within the context and made clear by solid biblical exposition.

I know many of my statements to this point have been direct and assume certain Calvinistic positions that I have addressed. Setting expectation up front is important to prevent misunderstanding; we see this practice throughout the Bible (so I have a good model to follow). The expositional portion of this book is a commentary on Romans 9; however, it is not that alone, but also an attempt to rescue these well-known passages from the Calvinistic presuppositions that often go unchallenged. I have a large library with both Calvinistic and non-Calvinistic authors that address Romans 9 and/or some related subject it covers, and all have been of value to me personally. Some Calvinistic authors were a great benefit to me since I became a Christian in 1982. Initially I did not know the various theological perspectives, and therefore read all without any particular scrutiny. Today I understand the differences, yet I can still read Calvinistic authors in a way that I benefit from their insight, even though they have positions I disagree with.

I find it interesting that many Calvinists can be quite insightful when commenting on texts not directly related to Calvinism. However, they manifest some inconsistency, for they tend to violate their own Calvinistic presuppositions through their insightful and helpful applications. Why is this? Because they often interpret incidental passages relating to man's responsibility in the clearest light of what the text says, which is commendable. They interpret God's appeal to sinners as legitimate, and man's response (if they stay true to the text) according to the normal reading. That is, man exercises faith or rebels against God of their own accord, and not determinatively. However, if they interpret the whole Bible through the Calvinistic lens, it makes no sense no matter what passages they choose and the beneficial insight vanishes. More often, they tend to keep their theology safely tucked away nearby so they can draw it out when needed to explain away man's free will, but they cannot remain consistent with the text if they do. This results in a back and forth, seemingly ad hoc, inconsistent hermeneutic as they strive to maintain loyalty to their deterministic system while developing insightful applications. Since the Bible does not match with their system of determinism, it leaves them with an impossible task of harmonizing Calvinistic theological contradictions. I believe this is because when it comes to real life, Calvinism in most aspects is not biblical, logical or practical. You can believe Calvinism, but you cannot consistently live Calvinism's ideals. Almost every Calvinistic interaction with the world outside of the Reformed pulpit requires a qualifying conversation, judgment, decision or response that is in conflict with the foundational premise of their deterministic theology.

Following the Calvinistic method consistently will result in the entire Bible saying something different from what it does plainly say. "One does not read long from the apologists for

Calvinism before finding them resorting to all manner of ingenious interpretations and applications in an effort to bolster their tottering theology."[52] Calvinists treat the Scriptures similar to Modalists, who put God in a position of logical absurdity, scriptural conflict, and grammatical distortion. Modalism[53] is a scriptural indignity and distorts the nature and character of God – not to mention it is a heresy. The Modalist describes God as performing a ventriloquist act in speaking to Himself, when appearing in different "modes" (Father, Son or Spirit). It would be analogous to someone wearing different masks at different times to manifest themselves as different people. Modalism is not a new heresy; Tertullian (2nd Century Latin church father) said against Praxeas the Monarchian (Monarchianism was essentially Modalism, rejecting the trinity) regarding his confusion of the nature of God, "He who speaks; and He of whom He speaks, and to whom He speaks, cannot possibly seem to be One and the Same. So absurd and misleading a statement would be unworthy of God."[54] Similarly, Calvinists teach God sovereignly controls every thought and act of man to the extent it creates the same problem, only from a different perspective. For example, the Bible teaches God is angry with man because of wicked deeds, but deterministically speaking, that makes God the One causing the person to do those deeds— this is absurd. If God is determining all aspects of man's decisions and behaviors, He is logically working against Himself since He ends up solving the problems He apparently (according to consistent Calvinists) creates. But this thoroughly misrepresents God's character. I agree with Tertullian; this view of God's nature is "unworthy of God." The Calvinist, like the Modalist, puts God into a position of logical absurdity and scriptural conflict, and toys with the grammar attempting to interpret the Bible coherently. What I am not saying—I want to be clear—is that Calvinism is a heresy like Modalism. Both theological systems put God in conflict with Himself; however, they do it for very different reasons. I believe Calvinism's fault lies in the determinism they impose on God resulting in an inconsistent interpretation of many passages of Scripture. In contrast, the God of Modalism is not the God of the Bible in essence or being. Calvinism redefines sovereignty and therefore understands God's acts deterministically. Thus, God within a Calvinistic framework acts in a way that I believe is unworthy of God, and this distorts aspects of His nature and character. But what Calvinism does not do (which Modalism does), is redefine the essence of God's being to create an entirely different god. Calvinists understand God's acts—what He does— deterministically, but this is not necessarily a heresy for at times God does act deterministically; it is a misjudgment of how He performs His acts in relation to man's freedom. Indeed, this is the very misjudgment I argue against in this book. This is because I believe God is truthful and does not deceive; therefore, His word will not lie nor will His methods be deceptive. The apologists of Calvinism will make various and sundry arguments in defense of their theology, but no matter what they contend, they can never escape the problem of distorting God's nature and character in the process.

In variance to Calvinism, Modalism changes the very essence of God's being as described in the Bible, which makes it a heresy. It describes God as a different being than the Bible says He is. This is no different from the Jehovah's Witnesses (JWs) that describe Jesus as Michael the ArchAngel. Since Jesus is not Michael the ArchAngel, their claim changes Jesus from who the Bible says He is (the eternal Son of God, second Person of the trinity) to an angel which He is specifically differentiated from (Heb. 1:5). Thus, JWs change the essence of the Son of God's being, which makes their view of Jesus heretical and defines the JW's as a cult. Jesus is not an angel that God the Father created; He is the eternal Son of God and Creator (John 1:1-3). On the other hand, Calvinists do not change the essence of God's being, but they change His acts to cause them to be unnatural and conflicting. I am not sure that any of us truly *comprehend* God, but the Scriptures certainly give us the ability to *apprehend* Him. I do not fully comprehend how the Son of God can add humanity to His deity, but I believe it and the evidence reveals it. Thus, I can apprehend Jesus in this way, though I cannot comprehend Him. But I apprehend Him by allowing the Bible to tell me what I need to know about God as He is revealed. I do not have the right to impose on God my own philosophical perspectives if they are at variance with the text; this I believe is the mistake of Calvinism. They have tried to take Calvin's view of God and interpret the Bible through that lens; however, that lens is a distorted one and it yields an inaccurate picture of God's nature and character, which in turn misjudges His acts.

The essential problem why many Calvinists today lack the ability to comprehend their own system is because it teaches one thing, but its application is another. They are seemingly unable to recognize the logical and scriptural contradictions of their theology, so they redefine terms to a palatable acceptance for themselves as well as others. They desire to hold to Calvinism and its Reformed status with a romantic loyalty, but it puts them in a quandary. Something has to give when they interpret their own system with intellectual honesty. Either they have to abandon their unreasonable theological presuppositions (which would mean a denial of Calvinism), or they have to redefine it so it does not look like what it in fact is—a logical contradiction and biblical dodging of the context. It is a classic picture of denial resulting in self-deception. And self-deception is the worst kind of deception. This results in many Calvinists applauding the king's "new clothes..." (Calvinist theology), though all the evidence reveals the contrary—"the king is naked"!

Determinism is an ancient philosophy that is fatalistic and filled with logical and philosophical contradictions. Using determinism as a philosophical lens to interpret the Bible and God's nature muddies up the biblical waters and removes any clarity in the Scriptures.

Finally, when exercising our hermeneutic, we are obligated to study the Bible with the self-evident principles discussed. People read all kinds of literature in the normal fashion, recognizing genre and discovering the meaning of the authors with the same hermeneutic promoted here. For some strange reason, when it comes to the Bible, people think that all logic and reason should go out the window and only a "mystical" or "spiritual" understanding is paramount. But this is a foolish mistake. For example, the Bible in both the OT and NT commands us "do not steal" (Exodus 20:15, Rom. 13:9). How am I to understand this simple command? The obvious answer is that I should not steal. This isn't rocket science or splitting atoms. We do not need special Bible codes to unlock the meaning or mystical visionary meanings to plain texts of Scripture. We should not be approaching the Bible allegorically as if we need to supply our own context and meaning to understand it. We need to understand it as Jesus and the Apostles did, in a literal (normal) manner (which includes similes, metaphors, figures of speech and other literary techniques). We certainly cannot improve on the Son of God in His view of Scripture. He interpreted Scripture in a normal (literal) manner, whether the texts were prophetic or non-prophetic. Therefore, we need to follow His lead, not only modeling His life, but also His biblical hermeneutic. He is our Lord!

REDISCOVERING LOGIC

The last piece we need to examine before the exposition of Romans 9 is the use of *logic* in our approach to the Bible. Everyone uses logic whether they realize it or not. Logic is not just a study of *formulistic* thinking methods; it is the *normal* thinking method used all the time. The question then becomes, are we using good or bad logic? The biblical writers (moved by the Holy Spirit) assume readers use their God-given human reason to comprehend their words. When David says, "The heavens are declaring the glory of God, and their expanse shows the work of his hands. Day after day they pour forth speech, night after night they reveal knowledge. There is no speech nor are there words — their voice is not heard — yet their message goes out into all the world, and their words to the ends of the earth" (Psalm 19:1-4, ISV), the assumption is that all people can see the created stars, planets, and handiwork of God. It assumes that all the world can see the same thing in the heavens and decipher the message that God is glorified by His creation. Of course, He has to exist to create the universe and put it on display for us to see. And what an amazing work it is—free cinema viewing for all the world, displaying His glorious handiwork; it only costs some time and thought.

It is only logical that if something is created, it requires a creator. If something is designed, it requires a designer. The cosmos had a beginning; therefore, it requires a Beginner. The Beginner of time, space, and matter cannot be part of time, space, and matter; in other words, the Creator must transcend or be beyond His creation. He cannot be what He creates, which is self-evident. Since the universe had a beginning, the Beginner or Creator of the universe must possess characteristics beyond that of the created order. We logically conclude as the Psalmist states, that this Being is eternal, non-material, intelligent, powerful, purposeful, non-contingent (does not require the created order to exist), and separate from His creation. All these are necessary characteristics of the Creator of the universe that the whole world can discover by simply observing the heavens. Expanding on this theme, Paul the apostle says in Romans 1:20: "From the creation of the world His invisible attributes, that is, His eternal power and divine nature, have been clearly seen, being understood through what He has made. As a result, people are without excuse" (HCSB). Why are people "without excuse" when it comes to recognizing God's existence? "Because what can be known about God is plain to them, because God has made it plain to them" (Rom. 1:19, NET). God has provided man with the ability to reason these things out by examination with the innate logic and reasoning ability He put in man. Now if man can deduce by logical reasoning the existence of a Creator of the universe through general revelation, and extrapolate the characteristics He must possess by that same reasoning process, special revelation (the Bible) will significantly add to and explain the creation. The writers of Scripture assume this kind of logical reasoning used to observe the heavens and draw these conclusions. It is impossible to overlook this fundamental thinking principle when reading the Bible or any other book— every writing assumes it—especially God's word (you are using it to comprehend what I am writing in this book). Further, in Romans 12:1, Paul said, "I beseech you therefore, brethren, by the mercies of God, that ye present your bodies a living sacrifice, holy, acceptable unto God, which is your reasonable service." The word "reasonable" is the Greek word *logikos* from which we get our English word *logic*. In other words, Paul says it is only "logical" that we "present ourselves" to God for service after all He has done for us, which he develops in the previous chapters of Romans. The logic is natural, clear, and simple.

Now before I am accused of putting too much emphasis on logic and reason, as mentioned, these are necessary when reading this or any other book. For example, in order to read the English Bible I have to understand enough about the English language to read it; this again is self-evident. This is true for any book written in the English language. Moreover, when reading the Bible it would be a great advantage to know both Hebrew and Greek, since these are the original languages. However, if I do not know those original languages, I can take advantage of the grammatical resources available to help understand the essential word definitions and grammatical rules of those languages. To claim at this point that I am putting too much of a premium on language would be absurd. The better I know the original language of the writers and the translation language I am reading, the better I can understand the Bible. It is the same principle when we use our logical thinking and reasoning ability when reading the Bible. Since the writers utilize logic, reason, and literary devices (analogies, similes, metaphors, contrasts, symbols, parables, comparisons, et al.), my understanding of these prior to reading the Bible will enhance my understanding of a writing, not diminish it.

When we approach the topic of reasonable thinking and examination, we come to what in formal logic is called the "law of non-contradiction." This is a self-evident thinking method that everyone uses, but within the discipline of logic, this label identifies it in distinction from other methods. The law of non-contradiction states, "two things cannot be opposite and true at the same time and in the same sense." In other words, I cannot be 6 feet tall and 4 feet tall at the same time and in the same sense. I can be 6 feet tall if *standing* and 4 feet tall if *sitting*, but sitting and standing are not the same sense. Moreover, I cannot both sit and stand at the same time. This is obvious, and people use this self-evident thinking method without trying because our Creator naturally builds it into us—He made us in His image (Gen. 1:27, 9:6). When people recognize it as a consistent way to think, they easily sense it all the time; it is unavoidable because it is so noticeable. This thinking should permeate everything we do, and it typically does. Yet when it comes to reading the Bible, unfortunately many Christians cast off logical thinking as they would a coat in flames. Some Christians actually consider it more spiritual to abandon reasoning skills and use a mystical approach to the Scriptures. They reason that it is a spiritual book, so it takes some kind of spiritual approach to discover its meaning. However, people that claim it is not spiritual to use logic or reason to understand the Bible are using logic and reason to argue against its use. This fact eludes them. If we ask what the mystical or spiritual approach is, the response would be almost as varied as the number of practitioners. In other words, there isn't one! Using logic and reason is the spiritual approach since the authors used it when they wrote and God created our thinking ability to comprehend it.

Other Christians would argue that using logical thinking is placing a premium on human reasoning. This could not be further from the truth and evidence of the second severely flawed approach to the Bible since anything I know about the Bible or read in the Bible necessitates I use human reason to understand it, of course not discounting the aid of the Holy Spirit illuminating it. Indeed, Jesus said the Spirit of God "will convict the world of sin, and of righteousness, and of judgment" (John 16:8, NKJV). Thus, His goal through the gospel is to make the truth understandable, bring people to faith in Christ, and thereby glorify Jesus (John 16:14a).

Logical thinking is necessary to comprehend Bible commands or the gospel itself. Returning to the previous example of the Bible's command "do not steal" (Exodus 20:15) is a good example. Reading that command requires I understand what it means *not* to steal, and the logical opposite of that command, which *is* to steal. This is the normal way we think and reason through any kind of command so we can understand them. Everything we read--inside and outside the Bible--passes through our mind so we can think, using our imagination in the process of analysis. To assume our reasoning ability is wrong to use is logically self-defeating, for we have to use it and the law of non-contradiction to argue against it. When you use a thinking method like non-contradiction to say you should not use that method, the statement fails to make sense because it violates its own truth principle that it claims. In other words, I cannot use logical principles to argue against using logical principles, that is self-defeating. When reading the Bible, I cannot throw aside logical thinking and assume it is spiritual to do so. If I do that, I have reasoned logically that I should not use logical thinking (self-contradiction) and opted for a method called "spiritual" that has no absolute basis to determine its meaning. In other words, if I abandon logic and reason, while using logic and reason to do it, not only am I contradicting myself, but whatever method I then replace it with I have reasoned its use. This is folly of the highest sort. For what am I to use as an absolute measurement to know this new thinking method is of any value? If it is isolated to my own whims and private wishes, I have committed the grossest error warned against, which is reasoning after my "own conceit" (Prov. 18:11, 26:5, 12, 16, 28:11). In other words, when people isolate their thinking to private principles to analyze and reject the normal logic Scripture writers assume, they create a moving target as the basis of their own made up logic. The result being interpretations that are also privately isolated to themselves (2 Peter 1:20), which have no connection to the context of the passage. In other words, the interpretation of the Bible can mean whatever the reader decides, for there is no standard available as a measurement.

The point here is that since the Holy Spirit is the real author behind the men who penned Scripture, the principles of logic will not be violated in the writings. Logic is grounded in the nature of God; therefore, He will not violate those logical principles when He communicates through His word. Indeed, the Bible will not teach contrary to what man can reasonably understand; otherwise, no one would really know what the Bible taught. The reasoning process we are discussing is not the same as, nor does it replace, the illumination the Holy Spirit gives a person when reading the Bible for insight and application. Indeed, they work in combination. For example, I can understand the logical reasoning of Paul when he makes a case for the justification of believers by faith in Galatians 3. There he correlates the blessing of faith with the promise given to Abraham (Gal. 3:14), and contrasts it with the law which brings a curse that Christ redeemed us from (Gal. 3:13). He then gives an everyday illustration in how contracts are binding agreements between people which others cannot disannul or alter (Gal. 3:15). Therefore, he concludes that the covenant of the law that came 430 years after the promise cannot disannul it and make it of no effect (Gal. 3:16-18). These two covenants (promise and law) are entirely different in the reasons for their creation and the effects of their operation. The promise made to Abraham and its blessings were received by faith; the law was established for a different purpose. The blessings contained in it are only received by obedience to its commands. One of the main reasons for the law was to define sin and reveal people's transgressions, with the educational result that the law did not *replace* the need for a Savior, indeed, it should have *established* it (Gal. 3:20-26). Anyone can read these verses and follow the logic of Paul as he develops the argument that Christians are not under the Law of Moses in their relationship with God. However, that does not mean that the unsaved person can comprehend the significance of the truth presented; that requires the illumination of the Holy Spirit (1 Cor. 2:14). Once a person is redeemed (born again), the Holy Spirit takes up residence in their life and becomes their ultimate Bible teacher (1 John 2:27). Now again, this does not mean that the church does not need Bible teachers, for one of the Spiritual Gifts is that of teachers and teaching (Rom. 12:7; Eph. 4:11). What it does mean, is that unless a person is regenerated by the Holy Spirit (Titus 3:5), and crossed over from death to life (John 5:24), that the truth taught in Scripture will not have significant meaning or the intended application, even if taught clearly by a Bible teacher.

The illumination that the Holy Spirit gives believers is essential to insightful application of the Bible for spiritual development. The unbeliever does not have this viewpoint, nor is able to make sense of the Bible in a significant and applicable way. Certainly, they can follow the logic and reason for much of what the Bible teaches, but it ends there. This is why the gospel is *preached* to unbelievers and the Bible is *taught* to believers. Believers require instruction and insightful application in the development of their relationship with Jesus Christ. The unbeliever has no relationship with Christ and is entirely unaware of the spiritual world that exists around them since they have been blinded by their unbelief that Satan takes full advantage of (2 Cor. 4:4). Simply put, an unbeliever can understand the command to not kill (Exodus 20:13; Deut. 5:17), but the believer does not simply understand the command but also realizes the significance of the command in their relationship and accountability to God. The Holy Spirit moves in the heart of the *believer* convicting to love and please God, but the Holy Spirit works with the *unbeliever* to bring about the conviction of their sin and their need for a Savior (John 16:8), which the believer already has. Thus, we have two entirely different perspectives. From the believer's perspective, they are developing a relationship with Jesus and growing in a life of holiness with the aim of pleasing and glorifying God. The unbeliever is void of these concerns and is uninterested in pleasing or glorifying God because there is no relationship. If anything, the unbeliever will have personal, selfish motives for using the Bible (if they do at all), or simply try to appease God as pagans would the gods of the pagan world—to get Him off their back and pacify any anger they believe may be present. Though Christians can deteriorate into this kind of similarly distorted relationship with God, it is not the normal course or basis of their relationship as the NT describes.

We are told in Proverbs 3:5 not to lean on "your own understanding." But how do you *know* what "your own understanding" is unless you can logically contrast it with the understanding that the Bible provides? There has to be a way to know the difference between the two methods of understanding; otherwise, the only option left is to trust myself instead of God which places confidence in the wrong area—my "own conceit." There is no way to avoid the use of the reasoning ability God created in us no matter how you slice it, specifically when it comes to trusting in, or having faith in God. This is because "faith cometh by hearing, and hearing by the word of God" (Rom. 10:17). Therefore, the word of God that enters my ears, has to make sense to my mind to reach my heart, resulting (hopefully) in faith exercised of my will—the ultimate goal. G. Campbell Morgan rightly said, "...faith is not merely intellectual apprehension and conviction of truth; and shows that faith is the assent of the will, and the yielding of the life, to the claim of the truth of which the mind is convinced."[55]

Why do we have to use logic and reason when reading the Bible? Should we not just read it and do what it says and leave it there? To understand logic and reason is in the realm of epistemology[56] and is a start. However, we need to take a further step to ask the question why logic and reason exist in the first place, which is the ontological[57] question. God created man in His image with the capability to reason, which comes from Him. God created man with the ability to gain knowledge, analyze the facts of that knowledge, and reason it out to a proper use, or what we call wisdom. But logic and reason need to be grounded somewhere other than in man's subjective mind. They are grounded in the mind of God and find their perfection in Him. Further, we understand from this that God will not do anything that is not logical. For example, God will not make a rock too big for Him to lift or make a square circle—these are logical impossibilities. Additionally, God is not subject to the laws of logic as if they are something outside of Him and imposed on Him. The laws of logic are grounded in the nature of God. Thus, when God communicates through the Scriptures, He assumes the use of logic and reason so there can be understanding and application. To avoid these innate abilities in man abandons the purpose for God infusing them into the fabric of human nature in the first place.

Having said that, the exposition of Romans 9, as well as any other Scripture requires the use of logic in their analysis. God will not violate logical thinking when communicating; therefore, the writers of Scripture—led by the Holy Spirit— will not. This means that we cannot look at the Scripture in a way that would logically contradict reality, or contradict itself in other comparative Scripture references. Since God logically uses various literary devices through the biblical writers, we need to understand the Scriptures without altering them to match a preconceived theological concept, but instead, draw our theological concepts from the Bible.

The Bible reveals things in the NT that are a "mystery," but this simply means that what is communicated would never be understood unless revealed (i.e. by revelation). The NT church (Jews and Gentiles in one Body in Christ) is one such mystery (Eph. 3:3-9). Mysteries were events not prophesied in the OT and therefore only understood by revelation in the NT. Mysteries in this sense cannot be understood by searching or discovering by clues, but only by revelation. Certainly, there are mysteries —not in the NT sense—which are things mysterious to us because we lack the ability to completely comprehend certain aspects of reality, but this is different. For example, the Bible teaches me that God is a Trinity or Tri-Unity, thus I cannot completely understand how God who is an eternal, infinite Being actually exists, never mind the Tri-Unity of His Being. I can understand what the Bible says about Him and believe it, but I cannot completely comprehend God. If I could, I would be a bit concerned—I am finite and He is infinite. Therefore, there is an aspect in my understanding in which God is a mystery to me since I lack complete comprehension. However, because I know what the Bible reveals about God, I can worship Him and know what He wants me to know about Him. He has revealed enough of His nature and characteristics to us that we can recognize His awesome ability and love for us. Therefore, when I use the term mystery in the exposition in Romans 9, there is a discernible difference between what the NT calls a mystery and a mystery in the sense that it is something I will never completely understand because of my human limitation—such as the Trinity. This distinction is important because Calvinists often appeal to *mystery* (not the NT sense) when they have logical and scriptural contradictions in their doctrines. Indeed, the only real mystery at that point is how they can maintain their blatantly inconstant views.

Finally, we read instructions all throughout the Bible that demand we use our reasoning ability to understand. For example, Deut. 13 instructs how to logically examine the claim of a prophet or dreamer of dreams. It requires making a logical comparison between what Moses previously wrote and the claim made by the alleged prophet or dreamer. The thinking process necessary for this is a logical examination of the claim by comparing it to the Scriptures to discover coherence or conflict. This requires a process that involves our ability to exercise our faculty of reason. In other words, is the statement made by the prophet or dreamer in line with and correlate to what Moses previously wrote, or is it in conflict? It also requires a conclusion to be drawn that determines whether the prophet or dreamer of dreams is to be believed or stoned. Not a trivial decision.

In another example, Deut. 17:14-20 instructs about laws concerning kings. A king was not to multiply horses, wives, or silver and gold. There is a specific reason why kings should not multiply wives (other than the obvious sin of adultery); there is the danger of the kings' heart turning away from God (Deut. 17:17). Many kings had political marriages with women from foreign countries to negotiate peace between nations. No king (it was thought) would invade a country that housed his daughter and grandkids. This may provide security for the king having married a neighboring king's daughter, but with the addition of these wives was the addition of the worship of foreign gods these women brought with them. This was a violation of God's intention of marriage from the beginning (Mark 10:6), which is one man for one woman for one life. Nevertheless, many nations had kings who multiplied wives for political expediency, pleasure, and offspring. The point here is that Moses gave the *reason* for the command, which requires our reasoning ability to understand it, since it provides the potential danger of its violation. In the instruction, Moses provided the reason: "neither shall he multiply wives to himself, that his heart turn not away." History informs us that Solomon started out exercising great wisdom as Judah's king after his father David. But he eventually violated this command bringing upon himself and Israel the disastrous consequences warned of beforehand (1 Kings 11:4). Ironically, with all the wisdom Solomon displayed when appealing to logic and reason throughout the book of Proverbs, he did not personally heed them. Sadly, there is example after example in the OT for the logical reason to obey various commands when confronted. God provides reasons based on the consequences of disobedience and the blessings of obedience. God pleads with Israel through the prophets, offering godly wisdom in the book of Proverbs, and future encouragement through the multitude of messianic prophecies. With all these instructive reasons to maintain our faith in God through various life circumstances, like Solomon we can still end poorly. We all face the danger of not thinking clearly when reasoning through the instructions in Scripture; we can all fall like Solomon if we do not take heed to what is easily understandable and reasonable in its appeal.

A NT example should suffice to make the point. In Matt. 22:41-46, Jesus asked the Pharisees a question. In verse 42, Jesus said, "What do you think about the Christ? Whose Son is He?" The Pharisees answered, "The Son of David." In the next verse, Jesus asked them a question that required their reasoning out the answer by evaluating what the Scripture said. He asked, "How then does David in the Spirit call Him 'LORD'"? Jesus did not give them the answer directly, but quoted Psalm 110:1 and left it to them to reason it out. The only logical conclusion is that the Christ had to be more than human for David to refer to him in the Psalm the way He did. There is example after example throughout the NT. The epistles are logical arguments about doctrinal issues providing specific conclusions, using the absolute truth of Scripture as the measurement.

Every truth and command of Scripture assumes and requires our logical approach to both understand them and to apply them. It is inescapable! When David proclaims in Psalm 19 "the heavens declare the glory of God," he is basing that on the God-given ability to look to the heavens and know that they did not get there without God creating them. He was making the claim founded in the early chapters of Genesis to be sure. But we know that it is more than that, for in verses 3 and 4b he says, "There is no speech nor language, where their voice is not heard. Their line is gone out through all the earth, and their words to the end of the world." This message is throughout the world—beyond Israel who had the written word to those who did not. It was the heavens that God provided as a general revelation to speak of His existence and glory. Paul the apostle confirms this in Romans 1:20: "...the invisible things of him [God] from the creation of the world are clearly seen, being understood by the things that are made..." This general revelation of creation that all the world can see in the heavens and on earth, witness to God's eternal power and intelligence, so much so that Paul declares, "so that they are without excuse." Why is that? "Because what may be known of God is manifest in them, for God has shown it to them" (v. 19, NKJV). God has created man with the reasoning ability to look at what is before their eyes and conclude the only logical cause for the existence of all things is God. Man has to evade every built-in instinct, reasoning ability, and innate power of deduction to avoid this truth. However, this is exactly what we observe in the writings and claims of atheists today. They live in a constant willful delusion of conflicting statements and illogical conclusions to maintain their atheistic position. Anyone with a little bit of sense and thoughtful consideration can see it, except the atheists in their blind commitment to materialism.[58] Just as Paul said in Romans 1:21b, they "became futile in their thoughts, and their foolish hearts were darkened" (NKJV). I cannot find a more apt statement of the irrational claims and self-contradictory arguments of today's atheists and their nonsensical conclusions. As bad as this is, it is to be expected. However, it should not be something we see among thinking Christians who read and study the Bible. Yet, we do see this as Calvinistic presuppositions force illogical and unreasonable conclusions on the Scriptures because contrary views would violate John Calvin's views. The results are a distortion of the nature and character of God.

REDISCOVERING INTERPRETIVE PRINCIPLES

In preparing for the expositional section of this book, examining the nature and character of God provides a framework for the interpretations to follow. To understand the nature of God, it is easier to begin with certain attributes of God. An attribute of God is something that God possesses because of His nature. For example, because God's nature is holy, holiness is an attribute He possesses. Therefore, any attribute possessed by God because of His nature, reveals His nature. Calvinism alters the description of some of God's attributes because of their theological presuppositions—the premise of this book. Therefore, having a perspective on the nature and character of God is integral when analyzing how Calvinists deviate in these aspects. I will attempt to point this out in specifics in the actual exposition of Romans 9.

God is infinite (no finite limitations) eternal (without beginning or end), all knowing (omniscient), all-powerful (omnipotent) and everywhere (omnipresent). These are intrinsic to His nature as the only infinite, eternal, all-powerful, all knowing, everywhere-present Being. These are revealed in the following table so Calvinistic perspectives can be measured against the Bible's revelation of them. The following table lists biblical attributes (not exhaustive) and their relation to Calvinism:

TABLE 1 (ATTRIBUTES OF GOD'S NATURE)

ATTRIBUTES INTRINSIC TO GOD'S NATURE	CALVINISTIC *DEVIATION*	SCRIPTURE REFERENCE
Eternal	No Deviation	Psalm 147:5
Immutable	No Deviation	Malachi 3:6
Omniscient	Omniscient <u>because</u> He *determines* the future	Psalm 147:5
Omnipotent	No Deviation	Genesis 1:1, Jer. 32:27
Omnipresent	No Deviation	Psalm 139:7, Col. 1:17
All-wise	No Deviation	Job 12:13
Holy	No Deviation	Lev. 11:44
Loving	Loves *elect* has less love for non-elect	1 John 4:16
Righteous	No Deviation	Psalm 89:14
Truthful	*Questionable*--God does not make *genuine* offers	Exodus 34:6, Num. 23:19, Heb. 6:18
Morally Perfect	No Deviation	Psalm 86:5

In addition to God's nature, He possesses characteristics that are associated with His character, and these are in relation to His creation--man in particular. For example, sovereignty is a characteristic of God and associated with His nature, but sovereignty only exists because of His relationship to His creation; He is sovereign over it. Apart from His creation, God does not exercise sovereignty for there is no one to reign over. From these types of characteristics, we can discover the character of God. What is key regarding God's character is to correlate His revealed character based on His nature which can only be understood from His word, not any presuppositions external to the Bible. Again, taking sovereignty as an example, God's nature is loving, merciful, truthful, etc., so from this we conclude that He will exercise His sovereignty in acts that will align with His nature. These acts will not violate any of His attributes. God will never be unloving, lie, or be unmerciful. His mercy may reach an end because of a time element or situational opportunity to repent, but His nature regarding mercy does not change. As Paul said, "And the times of this ignorance God winked [Greek: huperiedo = overlook, not punish; Strongs #G5237] at; but now commandeth all men every where to repent: Because he hath appointed a day, in the which he will judge the world in righteousness by that man whom he hath ordained; whereof he hath given assurance unto all men, in that he hath raised him from the dead" (Acts 17:30-31). Therefore, until that "day"—or a person's death, or judicial hardening through rebellion—God's mercy is available to them.

God's mercy operates similarly to God's love in Calvinism. Calvinists do not believe God loves those He does not elect, and therefore only extends mercy to those He elects. It is no coincidence that love is the source of mercy; indeed they are woven together in the fabric of God's nature and character. A look at what the Bible reveals to us about God's mercy will aid greatly in our study here. It is essential for us to know what God tells us about His mercy to know how we can apply it to our knowledge of God.

To begin with, the Bible tells us that God's mercy endures forever in references such as: 1 Chron. 16:34, 41; 2 Chron. 5:13, 7:3,6, 20:21; Ezra 3:11; Psalm 107:1, 118:1-4, 29, 136:1-26 (repeated in every verse), 138:8; and Jer. 33:11. What is interesting to note in many of these verses, God's goodness is associated with His mercy. This point cannot be disregarded, for this word is used in the key verse (Exodus 33:19) which is quoted by Paul in Romans 9:15 and directly associated with God's exercise of mercy. Goodness describes the nature of God-- who He is! The word is used about 560 times in the OT (Hebrew usage) and expresses something that is beneficial, pleasing, desirous, and advantageous. It is used in contrast to something evil; therefore, man is told to do good and seek good (Psalm 34:14; Amos 5:14). But how would man know what *good* is? There must be an absolute measurement of what is good to know what to avoid as evil. Indeed, goodness is grounded in the nature of God. Since goodness is grounded in the nature of God, we can then see it expressed in His exercise of merciful acts towards man. God's nature is the source of His acts; therefore, we know His character by His acts and commands. These are NOT arbitrary; they express the very nature and character of God. There is consistency of what God reveals about Himself in Scripture and how He expresses Himself toward man. To obscure the reasons for the goodness and mercy of God toward man would result in a God of wavering unpredictability. Indeed, why would the Scripture spend so much time defining God as good and merciful, loving and kind, if the exercise of those attributes toward man were unpredictable? This question has yet to be given an adequate scriptural answer by Calvinists. The best Calvinists can do is follow Calvin's line of thinking and assign God's exercise of mercy to His will alone. However, from their perspective, since the reason for the exercise of mercy is not knowable, they are left with a relationship with God that is distant and unpredictable (if they are logically consistent). This is only because they ignore all other scriptural indications of why and how God shows mercy.

The Bible also reveals that God's mercy is new every morning (Lam. 23:22-23); this is tied to His faithfulness. Again, it must be asked in what way is God faithful? In the Lamentations text, God's faithfulness is seen in His covenant promise to Abraham regarding the Messianic redemptive blessing to the world, which had not yet occurred when Jeremiah was lamenting. He exclaimed in those verses that "it is of the LORD'S mercies that we are not consumed." Why is that? Because if Israel were consumed, God would have failed in His covenant promise to Abraham, and the redemptive aspect of that blessing to the nations would have ended at the Babylonian captivity. However, Jeremiah knew that God is faithful to His promises and covenant to the nation of Israel and therefore he could take comfort in that within the crisis of Jerusalem's destruction. Jeremiah knew it was not the end because the captivity would only last 70 years

(Jer. 29:10), and then God would bring them back to the land. All these themes run through the Bible and provide the background for Paul's theology when we get to Romans 9.

God's mercy can be knowable in its exercise to those who fear Him (Psalm 103:11, 17; Luke 1:50). Thus, He does not show His mercy capriciously, but in accordance with His truth and faithfulness which are secured in heaven (Psalm 36:5, 57:10, 89:2). The object lesson for this is the book of Jonah. Jonah certainly knew this about God and it is one of the main themes of the book. When Jonah was called to go to Nineveh, though a faithful prophet until that point (2 Kings 14:25), he rebelled at the call and took a boat in the opposite direction. The question is why he did everything possible to avoid going to Nineveh. The answer is the Assyrian nation, of which Nineveh was the capital. Jonah lived in northern Israel and was a prophet to the wicked and idolatrous kings of Israel's northern kingdom. Though the kings were evil, Jonah still had patriotic love for the nation of Israel. The Assyrians, well-known to the Jews and other nations for their cruelty and barbarism, were feared and despised. They were a merciless nation that had not known defeat at the time of Jonah's call to go to Nineveh. Jonah lived in the northern Galilee region of Israel; it is certain that Jonah at least knew of Israelites that had been terrorized or killed by the Assyrians and saw them as a vicious enemy that deserved the righteous judgment of God. The last thing Jonah was interested in was showing mercy to that wicked nation which is why he tried to flee to Tarshish. But Jonah learned his lesson and ended up at the shores of Nineveh, delivering the message God sent him there to give: "Yet forty days, and Nineveh shall be overthrown" (Jonah 3:4). However, Nineveh repented at the preaching of Jonah, both king and people; they even demonstrated their repentance in the animals (Jonah 3:6-10). God had mercy on them because of their repentance. This greatly angered Jonah (Jonah 4:1), and he said, "...was not this my saying, when I was yet in my country? Therefore I fled before unto Tarshish: for I knew that thou art a gracious God, and merciful, slow to anger, and of great kindness, and repentest thee of the evil" (Jonah 4:2). Yes, the mercy of God was not a mystery to Jonah. He knew that if the people repented, God would extend mercy. As Jonah said, that was why he immediately tried to flee to Tarshish (Spain), because he was not interested in seeing the Assyrians blessed, but destroyed. Indeed, this was the message of the book for the rebellious idolatrous kings in northern Israel of which Jonah had dealings. If God showed grace and mercy at the repentance of wicked Assyrians who brutalized Israel and other nations, why would He not do the same to His own people Israel if they repented? The compelling fact here is that Jonah knew that God would be merciful if Nineveh repented; there was no question in his mind. Indeed, it is why he initially fled from the call.

What are we to conclude from what the Bible reveals about God and His mercy? At a minimum, God will extend mercy to anyone who repents (Luke 18:13-14). Jesus made a point to criticize the Pharisees for their lack of mercy, and sent them back to the Bible to understand it: "But go ye and learn what that meaneth, I will have mercy, and not sacrifice" (Matt. 9:13a). Moreover, Jesus associated the topic of extending mercy with repentance when He said, "for I am not come to call the righteous, but sinners to repentance" (Matt. 9:13b). But the question at this point is how can they learn mercy in relation to repentance if it is only mysteriously concealed in the will of God and unknown to man? According to Calvinistic thinking, it appears that Jesus is asking the Pharisees to learn something unknowable to anyone. This is the crux of the issue with regard to God's character. Why is Jesus criticizing them for their mercilessness? Why is Jesus telling them to learn about how God offers mercy so they can properly represent Him? Is Jesus just making the statement for the record, knowing that they cannot ever really know why God shows mercy to anyone? Is Jesus commanding them to perform a task they are not able to perform? Would not this put Jesus in a questionable light regarding His own exercise of justice and mercy? These questions need adequate answers by Calvinists since they are the ones that impose the mystery and unpredictability on God's exercise of mercy. For without an adequate biblical explanation, it only distorts the nature and character of God. This is the danger of focusing an entire theological system on a verse or two, to the exclusion of all other relevant Scripture contexts that apply to the same subject.

The following table has characteristics that exist because God has a relation to His creation. Remember, God's character—how these characteristics operate—are grounded in His nature.

TABLE 2 (CHARACTERISTICS OF GOD TO CREATION)

CHARACTERISTIC REVEALING CHARACTER	CALVINISTIC OPERATIONAL *DEVIATION*	SCRIPTURE REFERENCE
Mercy	To *some* not all	Exodus 34:6
Wrath	None	Rom. 2:5
Justice	Overemphasis dominates and mitigates God's love	Psalm 19:9
Sovereign	Sovereign control because He *determines* all	Job 42:2, Psalm 115:3, 135:6

REDISCOVERING ROMANS OVERVIEW

The solution to rediscovering Romans 9 is to walk through the chapter in verse-by-verse exposition. However, it is important to keep in mind that the verses will reflect the context of the chapter, which is following the theme of the book of Romans. Paul establishes the theme in chapter 1:15-17, when he writes, "I am ready to preach the gospel to you that are at Rome also. For I am not ashamed of the gospel of Christ: for it is the power of God unto salvation to every one that believeth; to the Jew first, and also to the Greek. For therein is the righteousness of God revealed from faith to faith: as it is written, The just shall live by faith." The righteousness of God is revealed in the gospel. The gospel enables the imputation (transfer) of God's righteousness to man when he believes the gospel. Paul's goal is to reveal *why* the gospel is necessary and *how* the gospel is applied.

Paul uses the word *gospel* 13 times in 13 verses in Romans. From the very first verse, Paul says that he was "separated unto the gospel of God," thus the gospel is the overriding theme and movement of the epistle. He says, "I serve [God] with my spirit in the gospel of his Son" (1:9). He is "ready to preach the gospel" in Rome (1:15). He is "not ashamed of the gospel" (1:16) because "it is the power of God unto salvation," which is the issue behind the gospel itself. Later in chapter 10, he says, "How beautiful are the feet of them that preach the gospel" (10:15), focused on Israel in the immediate context. And the next verse says, "But they have not all obeyed the gospel" (10:16) and quotes

Isaiah in support. He speaks about his "ministering the gospel of God" (15:16), and how he "fully preached the gospel" (15:19). Moreover, he "strived to preach the gospel" (15:20) where others did not and wanted to "come in the fullness of the blessing of the gospel" (15:29) to Rome. Thus, we see that Paul kept the gospel as a theme throughout the entire letter. This cannot be removed from the context of any verse we look at regarding this epistle.

The major theme is the imputation (transfer) of God's righteousness to man through faith when the gospel is believed. However, there are also minor themes that run through the book which help make interpretive connections. For example, Paul connects Israel's responsible handling of the word of God in chapter 3:1-2, with the benefits that are provided when he mentions them in chapter 9:4-5. He also connects them to Romans 3:3-5 and, speaking of Israel's unbelief regarding that same word, with 9:6-7 connecting the same subtheme. The point is, chapter 9 is not written in isolation from the other chapters, nor should it be interpreted separately from them. When Paul brings up Israel's relation to their keeping of God's word in chapter 3, the thought in chapter 9 must be connected back to the initial introduction of the same thing. Remember, this is a letter without chapters in the original document, so we cannot allow the chapter breaks to break the letter and disjoint the context.

The key in this brief overview is that the writing is one letter, not separate topics written over a period of time. Paul addressed varying issues in the letter, but they all have a connective theme which is that God's *righteousness* is only attained through believing the gospel. Paul uses the word *righteousness* 39 times in 33 verses, again, an important aspect of this letter. Paul starts the letter by saying that God's righteousness is revealed (and imputed) through the gospel (1:16-17), but connects the word with other aspects of Christ's work of redemption. Short of quoting all 39 mentions of the word, a few are insightful regarding our present study. In chapter 9, Paul informs us "that Gentiles, who did not pursue righteousness, have attained to righteousness, even the righteousness of faith; but Israel, pursuing the law of righteousness, has not attained to the law of righteousness. Why? Because they did not seek it by faith, but as it were, by the works of the law" (9:30-32). This is a concluding statement by Paul to the argument he develops in Romans 9, so it provides us great insight into the points in the previous verses. Examining Paul's use of words throughout the epistle helps make a comparison of his usage.

At a high level, the book of Romans falls into the following basic outline:

Chapters 1-3a reveal that the whole world is under condemnation and in need of God's righteousness.

Chapters 3b-5a reveal the solution to condemnation, which is justification by faith. This is how God's righteousness is imputed.

Chapters 6-8a reveal the sanctification of the believer by being united with Christ and the power of the Holy Spirit,

Chapter 8b reveals the predestined glorification of the believer.

Chapter 9 reveals Israel's past election by God.

Chapter 10 reveals Israel's present rejection by God.

Chapter 11 reveals Israel's future restoration by God.

Chapters 12-16 are the chapters where Paul develops how believers apply what he taught them through the previous 11 chapters.

Introducing Romans 9 is important for setting the tone, and that is just what Paul the apostle does for us. Though some commentators cannot find a way for these chapters (9, 10, and 11) to fit into the flow of thought, they are very much part of Paul's theme. To misunderstand the overall theme of the letter would result in viewing a separation of chapters 9-11 as a detached subject. Commentators only detach them from the theme of the epistle because they are imposing a view on them that does not fit with their predisposition of Paul's teaching. Transitioning from chapter 8 where Paul emphasizes the believer's predetermined destiny to glory, and God's faithfulness in accomplishing it, he now continues with the key topic in question (the elephant in the room)—What about Israel? What is the relationship of Israel to the work of God through the church of Jesus Christ? Did God not make promises and a covenant with Israel? What will come of that—of them? Did God not use Israel as the vehicle to bring both the word of God and Messiah of God into the world? Yet, they have not received the very message God chose them to carry. Therefore, how was Paul to address this situation and prepare the Roman believers to "present" themselves to God in full confidence in chapter 12 (where the application of the letter begins)? Indeed this will be difficult if the question regarding Israel's status is not answered and the problem of Israel's present condition remains without conclusion.

Bearing in mind these questions and considerations, is God fair in His dealings with Israel? Does God even care about them? Did He just abandon them or is there something else that will explain their condition? Israel's current state of unbelief must be considered before chapter 12 begins. Therefore, Paul addresses all of these concerns and more in chapters 9-11. He not only answers the question, but also explains the problem in clear detail. The spoiler alert is that God has not cast off His people Israel, but will complete His promised plan in and through that nation.

REDISCOVERING
ROMANS 9

1 I say the truth in Christ, I lie not, my conscience also bearing me witness in the Holy Ghost, 2 That I have great heaviness and continual sorrow in my heart. 3 For I could wish that myself were accursed from Christ for my brethren, my kinsmen according to the flesh:

Paul now begins his next topic in Romans 9 by way of introduction through two *witnesses*, Paul's *conscience* and *the Holy Ghost* (God). Telling the *truth* regarding these witnesses is evidenced by a *great heaviness and continual sorrow* for Israel in Paul's *heart*. His concern is so great for them that he is willing—though not possible—to trade places with them for their national conversion. Paul always had a heart for the nation and this was evident by his yearning to reach Jerusalem and share the gospel with his fellow countrymen. When he finally reached Jerusalem, things did not work out the way he planned (Acts 21). He needed to be rescued from an angry Jewish mob who would have killed him if it were not for the intervening of Roman soldiers. Paul eventually ended up as a prisoner of Rome with, no doubt, discouragement based on the terrible course of events, but Jesus encouraged him (Acts 23:11) that his witness before the nation was what God wanted. Paul was responsible for delivering the message, not the results.

Indeed, this powerful desire and *heaviness* in Paul is contrary to Calvinistic determinism. If God determines the nation to reject the gospel, why is Paul appearing more loving in his concern for them than God? Moreover, why is Paul saying that the **Holy Ghost** (Spirit) is also **bearing witness** to this concern? Is Paul confused? Should we listen to the rest of what Paul has to teach if his concern for Israel is contrary to God's deterministic plan? This does not make any sense unless we try to frontload the Calvinistic presuppositions into the text, and thereby minimize Paul's words.

Paul's concern for the nation is similar to that of Moses in Exodus 32:30-35. This section of Exodus becomes key when Paul in verse 15 quotes from Exodus 33:19. In the exposition to follow, we will examine the context of the OT passages Paul references so we can remain in the contextual flow and argument of Paul's teaching.

4 Who are Israelites; to whom pertaineth the adoption, and the glory, and the covenants, and the giving of the law, and the service of God, and the promises;

Paul now defines his **kinsmen according to the flesh** as **Israelites**. He addresses Israel by their covenant name. Notice he does not call them Jews, since their ethnicity is not the issue, but the benefits the nation received under the covenant with God. **Adoption** is the first benefit listed and refers to the full benefits a child receives when they come of age. Israel as a nation enjoyed the benefits of God's relation with them as a son (Exodus 4:22). The **glory** was experienced exclusively by that nation as the Shekinah cloud would descend and God would speak to Moses (Exodus 24:16, 29:43). Israel enjoyed God's presence as no other nation did.

The **covenants** would amount to the *Abrahamic*, *Mosaic* and *Davidic* covenants. God's covenant with Abraham (Gen. 12-17, particularly chapter 15) amounts to a one-sided (unilateral) covenant God made with Abraham while he was asleep. The covenant guaranteed that God would accomplish three things: first, a large number of descendants through Abraham that would make up the nation of Israel; second, the land that God promised to give those descendants; and finally, the redemptive blessing that God would bring through Abraham to the benefit of all nations. This blessing was the Messiah, the Savior of the world. This redemptive promise would be refined and developed over time as we see that the Messiah would come through the tribe of Judah (Gen. 48:9-12), lineage of David (1 Sam. 7:12-16), born of a virgin (Isaiah 7:14), born in Bethlehem Ephrathah (Micah 5:2), and the time of His arrival (Daniel 9:25). Indeed, it would be very difficult to miss the arrival of this one so distinctly described and predicted.

The Mosaic covenant was next. This was a conditional covenant made with the nation which began in Exodus 19:5-8. The covenant is very specific and there were national blessings for keeping the covenant and national curses for breaking it (Deut. 27-28). This covenant did not replace the Abrahamic covenant, which is essential to understand God's historical managing of Israel as a nation. God fulfills the Abrahamic covenant without respect to anyone else, but the Mosaic covenant requires Israel's conditional obedience for its fulfillment. Important to note about these covenants is that Israel was under both these covenants simultaneously. This meant that the conditions of both covenants were applicable to the nation. Thus, at times God would have mercy on Israel enabling Him to continue the unilateral covenant through Abraham, but at other times He brought judgment and curse because Israel was in disobedience to the Mosaic covenant. Therefore, He extended mercy according to His will fulfilling the divine purpose for Israel, but when judgment was necessary He judged according to the Mosaic covenant. Yet He never destroyed or eliminated Israel because of His promise and plan which He worked through the Abrahamic covenant. However, their history of continued stubborn rebellion certainly warranted their judgment and even their destruction.

Next, we have the Davidic covenant (2 Sam. 7:12-16). Here God promises David that the Messiah would descend from his lineage. Finally, the New Covenant predicted in Jeremiah 31:31-34 which the church enters into because of their position "in Christ," which Israel will enjoy once they return to the

Lord (Rom. 11:15, 26-29). The evidence of their return will be their national conversion during the 7-year tribulation period (Rev. 6-18), which results in the bringing in of the Messianic thousand-year reign on earth (Rev. 19-20) and blessing on the world (Rom. 11:12, 15).

The *giving of the law* is a reference to the Law of Moses that greatly benefitted the nation. Christians at times tend to look at the law in a negative way through a history of misguided Bible teaching. However, the Law—though unable to be kept by Israel, or anyone else (Acts 15:10)—not only is a revealer of sin (Gal. 3:19), but was used by God to train the nation in preparation for the coming Messiah (Gal. 3:22-29). It taught the slaves that came out of Egypt how to be a nation, how to approach God, who God was in His holiness, and how they were to represent Him. It acted like a national constitution for them in spiritual, moral, and civil matters. It kept them separate from the dangers of paganism and idolatry which permeated the morally corrupt nations that encircled them. It revealed to them what was not otherwise knowable about God, man, the history of the world, the history of their nation, and His redemptive plan (Deut. 29:29).

The *service of God* was specific to approaching and worshipping God. The five offerings in the first seven chapters of Leviticus gave the specifics of how sinners were to approach this Holy God. God was not approachable by man's wisdom, preferences, or devices, but only by specifically prescribed methods. The violation meant death, which Aaron's sons learned (Lev. 10). Leviticus chapter 23 provides the seven feasts given as the means of staying right with or abiding in God as they celebrated that which God accomplished for them. The feasts were a remembrance of their history viewed through God's faithfulness and provision for them.

Finally, in this verse Paul mentions *the promises*. These would mostly regard the Messiah—who He would be and what He would accomplish. The OT is filled with prophecies and insightful descriptions of Him to make His arrival and activity highly recognizable. However, not all Israel recognized Him as the following verses show.

5 Whose are the fathers, and of whom as concerning the flesh Christ came, who is over all, God blessed for ever. Amen.

The *fathers* of the nation would be Abraham, Isaac, and Jacob, which Paul will discuss in the verses that follow. It was through the genealogy of these three fathers that the nation came into fruition and the Savior would arrive. Paul here emphasizes the Messiah's human body—*the flesh*—*came*, as Isaiah the prophet predicted, when he wrote the "child is born" (Isaiah 9:6a), in time. Moreover, he penned the "Son is given" (Isaiah 9:6b), indicating the Messiah is God since He came from heaven, in other words eternity. Paul makes the declaration that **Christ came who is over all, God**, which informs us that the Messiah was both God and man; One Person with two distinct natures. His deity is understood in distinction from His coming through the nation of Israel in His humanity.

Paul makes these points of Christ's humanity and deity in his opening of the epistle. He says that God "promised before through His prophets in the Holy Scriptures, concerning His Son Jesus Christ our Lord, who was born of the seed of David according to the flesh" (1:2-3), which establishes Jesus of Nazareth as the Messiah who fulfilled the prophetic requirements for His validation. The Messiah was always going to be fully human as the prophetic Scriptures made clear (Gen. 3:15). Moreover, the Messiah would be deity—the Son of God taking on a separate human nature, not combining the human and divine natures together. Thus, there are two natures in one Person. Not as Nestorianism taught, which was a fifth century heresy that divided the human person (Jesus) from the divine nature making two separate persons. This heresy taught that the second Person of the Trinity was not Jesus and did not die for our sins. Nor is it Monophysitism, another fifth century heresy that taught the divine nature and human nature of Christ intermingle and are confused into one nature.

Paul never confused the issue or natures, but kept the natures separate and made sure he presented the Son of God carefully. Notice he said Jesus was "…declared to be the Son of God with power according to the Spirit of holiness, by the resurrection from the dead" (1:4). Of the word *declared*, Thayer says "for although Christ was the Son of God before his resurrection, yet he was openly appointed [A.V. *declared*] such among men by this transcendent and crowning event."[59] Vincent says:

> There is an antithesis between *born* (Rom. 1:3) and *declared*. As respected Christ's earthly descent, He was born like other men. As respected His divine essence, He was declared. The idea is that of Christ's *instatement* or *establishment* in the rank and dignity of His divine sonship with a view to the conviction of men. This was required by His previous humiliation, and was accomplished by His resurrection, which not only *manifested* or *demonstrated* what He was, but wrought a real transformation in His mode of being.[60]

Finally, A. T. Robertson says:

> He was the Son of God in his preincarnate state (2 Cor. 8:9; Phil. 2:6) and still so after his Incarnation (Rom. 1:3, "of the seed of David"), but it was the Resurrection of the dead (*ex anastaseōs nekrōn*, the general resurrection implied by that of Christ) that definitely marked Jesus off as God's Son because of his claims about himself as God's Son and his prophecy that he would rise on the third day. This event (cf. 1 Corinthians 15) gave God's seal "with power" (*en dunamei*), "in power," declared so in power (2 Cor. 13:4). The Resurrection of Christ is the miracle of miracles.[61]

Therefore, Jesus was declared to be the Son of God and manifested to be so by His resurrection. Only deity could accomplish that miracle. The Messiah was deity prophetically (Psalm 2:7, 45:6,-7, 110:1; Prov. 30:4; Isaiah 9:6, 63:7, 9; Zech. 1:12, 12:10, 14:16), and Jesus Himself claimed He was deity (Mark 2:5-7; John 5:18, 23, 8:58, 10:30, a few examples). Now Paul claims it here, literally **Christ who is over all, God.**

6 Not as though the word of God hath taken none effect. For they are not all Israel, which are of Israel:

Notice Paul continues the contextual theme of the nation of Israel. In verse 3, he called them *kinsmen according to the flesh*, in verse 4, it was *Israelites*, and verse 5 *the fathers* (i.e. the start of the nation), with the emphasis on the Messiah's physical connection through that nation. Now in this verse the national theme continues.

Paul addresses here a misunderstanding held to by many Jews of his day. It is true that God elected Israel as a nation to a specific purpose, but it is not true that all the ethnic members of the nation were elected to salvation, the thrust of Paul's argument. Over the years, I have spoken to many people who claim to have "lost their faith" because of some circumstance in which God did not meet their expectation or answer some prayer the way they thought He should. But does this change God, His word, or the truth that Jesus rose from the dead? Of course not! If someone has a failed expectation because of a misunderstanding of God's response to a situation, this does not mean that God failed; the failure lies elsewhere. God is faithful to His promises and His people, whether national Israel or the church. The Bible is true and our particular perspective on it will never change that fact. The disillusionment of people because of misplaced expectations in God will never change the reality of who God is or how He acts.

Just because *the word of God hath taken none effect*, this does not change God's covenant promises to Israel, or anyone else for that matter. Paul introduced a similar discussion in chapter 3. After he explained how both Gentile and Jew were all guilty of sin and in need of God's righteousness through the first two chapters, he asks a question at the start of chapter 3, "what advantage does the Jew have"? In other words, if the Jew was just as guilty before God as a Gentile was, how did the Mosaic Law and rite of circumcision (sign of the Abrahamic covenant) in these covenant relationships advantage the Jew? Did not these provide some "advantage" in relationship with God? Paul answers by saying it was the "oracles of God" (the revelation of His word) that were committed to them (3:2). This was a privilege and great blessing to the nation, since it revealed God to them and instructed them in truth and righteousness. Within the revealed word was the promises made to Abraham, which was a guarantee God would always be with the nation. Moreover, His presence necessarily implied protection and advantage in the accomplishing of these promises. This advantage did not impute righteousness to them, but it instructed them in what righteousness was--as well as many other truths the pagan world did not have. Additionally, it delivered them from the grossly immoral practices of these pagan nations with the physical and mental illnesses of these self-destructive behaviors. But Paul asked, "...what if some did not believe"? Did "...their unbelief make the faithfulness of God without effect? Certainly not!" (3:3-4a, NKJV). Israel had the benefit of caring for the word of God, but their belief or unbelief did not change it. The main point Paul makes in chapter 3—which is essential to understanding his argument in chapter 9—is this; can the unbelief of Israel cause God to break His covenant with Abraham? "Certainly not!" God is faithful to His word and covenant promises no matter what man's response is to them. Man's faith does not affect God's faithlessness or cause His word to fail. This is exactly what Paul is reintroducing here in chapter 9, and it is a continuation of the same theme from chapter 3 regarding how God benefited Israel.

Israel had great benefits and privileges as listed in verse 5, but it does not logically follow that those benefits and privileges meant that every Israelite would believe them. *For they are not all Israel, which are of Israel,* in other words, not everyone in the nation of Israel believed God's word and had a saving faith. Though given the privilege of custodianship of the Scriptures, any unbelief or lack of trust in God meant that though genealogically a member of Israel, they were not true Israel, in other words possessing true faith. Indeed, if they rejected the word of God, they would not fulfill the definition of the name

Israel, which means to be a "prince with God" or to be "governed by God."

This verse is central going forward because Paul makes the comparison again of Israel regarding their unbelief and the gospel. The gospel began to be preached by Jews (apostles) and not only did Israel reject that message, but persecuted those preaching Christ (Acts 4:1-22, 5:17-42, 6:8-15, 7:54-60, 12:1-3, 14:19, 16:16-40, 17:5-14, 21:27-40). Paul wrote to the Thessalonians regarding the unbelieving Jews "Who both killed the Lord Jesus and their own prophets, and have persecuted us; and they please not God, and are contrary to all men: forbidding us to speak to the Gentiles that they might be saved, to fill up their sins alway: for the wrath is come upon them to the uttermost" (1 Thess. 2:15-16). With all the benefits God bestowed upon the Jews, for many it did not result in saving faith, but rather a filling up of their sins requiring God's wrath, not His blessing. The argument Paul develops here would make no sense in the framework of Calvinistic determination. If God sovereignly made some Jews believe and others reject the truth, why the appeal from the first verse? Indeed, why the chapter at all? Contrary to any Calvinistic presuppositions, Paul has not introduced anything remotely aligned with Calvinism, but only contrary perspectives thus far. To make the argument that Israel had many privileges provided to them only to have them ignored becomes meaningless if God *made* Israel ignore them, or (according to Calvinistic compatibilism) if God *ignored* them so they had no option to believe and did what their sinful nature desired. In any of the Calvinistic scenarios, Paul is wasting his time writing. It is abundantly clear that Paul possessed no hint of Calvinistic determinism in his theology. Therefore, any Calvinistic theology preloaded into Paul's writings or arguments is alien and therefore imposed. Essentially, to view Paul's statements in a Calvinistic framework proves a strong bias, since the text itself would have to be ignored to read that perspective into it. Thus, we continue on to the next verse as Paul builds his case.

7 Neither, because they are the seed of Abraham, are they all children: but, In Isaac shall thy seed be called.

After laying the foundation that not all in the nation of Israel possessed a true saving faith, Paul now steps back to the source of *genealogical* Israel—to **Abraham**. Simply put, not all of Abraham's children (**seed**, Greek *sperma*) were the line of God's choosing to bring both the word of God and Messiah of God to the world. Therefore, God's choice of Israel as the nation He would work through to bring salvation to the world was not by Abraham's decision to have a son through Hagar, but God's decision (choice) to have Abraham's son **Isaac** be in the Messanic line. Thus, it is **in Isaac** that Jesus Christ came into the world, not through Ishmael—the first physical child of Abraham. Back in Genesis 17, God promised a son to Abraham *and Sarah* when Abraham was one hundred years old and Sarah who was ninety and past childbearing years. At that point, Abraham already had Ishmael, "And Abraham said unto God, O that Ishmael might live before thee!" (Gen. 17:18). But God's response to Abraham there was significant and final; "God said: 'No, Sarah your wife shall bear you a son, and you shall call his name Isaac; I will establish My covenant with him for an everlasting covenant, and with his descendants after him. And as for Ishmael, I have heard you. Behold, I have blessed him, and will make him fruitful, and will multiply him exceedingly. He shall beget twelve princes, and I will make him a great nation'" (Gen. 17:19-20, NKJV). This is the issue Paul speaks about; God made His covenant with Abraham's son Isaac, not Ishmael. Therefore, Isaac is the means through which God chose to bring the redemptive blessing of the Messiah into the world. It was through Isaac and the nation of Israel, not through the line of Ishmael and the resulting nations of his line.

Paul reveals a parallel truth here. First, when he says not **all** the offspring of Abraham were **children**, he is referring to those of faith. Second, he emphasizes the key to the passage, that **Isaac** is the physical (national) choice for the line of the Messiah. It is God's choice of the line that brings salvation; neither man's choice nor effort have a place in this regard. Abraham's attempt to help God accomplish His purposes had disastrous consequences. The resulting birth of Ishmael produced an offspring that was a constant trouble to Israel and still is today. Man can never accomplish the salvation of God which Paul will discuss in later verses.

Paul develops this current issue further in Galatians 4:21-31 when he gives the illustration of Hagar and Sarah, comparing them to two Jerusalems. In his allegory, Paul shows that Hagar represented the Jerusalem in Israel, which was at that time bound under the Law of Moses. But Sarah represented the Jerusalem which is in heaven above and is free. Hagar represented the works of the flesh because it was Abraham's attempt to help God fulfill His promise with human effort instead of trusting God's word to him by faith—*in Isaac* the *seed be called*. Isaac was not only the second child (typical of the *second,* spiritual birth) but since both Abraham and Sarah were past childbearing years (Rom. 4:13-25, vv. 19-20 particularly) the birth was only due to God's miraculous intervention. Therefore, if God did not give Abraham the promise and fulfill it by His own divine power, there would be no nation of Israel and no messianic line. It is the same with salvation; it is not a work of man, it is the work of God initiated by God, accomplished by the power of God, and as a result, God is the One that is glorified. Which brings us to the next verse.

8 That is, They which are the children of the flesh, these are not the children of God: but the children of the promise are counted for the seed.

When Paul speaks of **promise**, he connects it to faith. Theologically Paul contrasts faith with works, and he contrasts law with grace. Faith is required to trust God for the promises He makes. You cannot earn a **promise**, nor can you earn grace. Promises, like grace, must be received, and to receive them faith is required. There is no measure of human works associated with faith because faith is trust from the heart, not works from human effort resulting in human merit. Calvinists make a grave error in attempting to define faith as a work or human merit. Jesus does not do it, Paul does not do it, and therefore we should not do it. There is no example in the Bible where faith is ever considered a work in relation to salvation.

The children of the flesh are those born of human effort, or works. This would be the case with Ishmael. Therefore, they are not the true *children of God*, but only those that came through the *promise* of God. A. T. Robertson says of this verse, "The children of the promise *(ta tekna tēs epaggelias)*. Not through Ishmael, but through Isaac. Only the children of the promise are "children of God" *(tekna tou theou)* in the full sense. He is not speaking of Christians here, but simply showing that the privileges of the Jews were not due to their physical descent from Abraham. Cf. Luke 3:8."[62] What Paul is not saying is that God chose certain people for salvation and others He did not. Paul is continuing his line of thought to express that the Messianic line is not because of human effort or merit, but it is God's sovereign choice of how He would bring the Savior to the world. The line or *seed* (sperma) is because of God's plan and power, not man's decision or capability. Paul continues to speak of Israel nationally, disclosing God's choice (election) and development of that nation. He is not speaking of certain Jews elected as individuals to salvation or others elected to be eternally lost. These concepts must be read into the text for they are foreign to Paul's line of argument. To add these alien theological constructs into the text entirely corrupts the meaning of it. Moreover, misunderstanding Paul's line of argument at this early stage only distorts the perspective as further into the chapter one goes. In other words, whatever misconceived notion is granted here not only must be maintained throughout the chapter, but must distort the interpretation of the further verses to keep the distorted continuity. Indeed, if I had a dollar for each time I've read or heard this done, I'd be a rich man.

9 *For this is the word of promise, At this time will I come, and*

Sara shall have a son.

Again, going to A. T. Robertson, the phrase **For this is the word of promise** is "Literally, "this word is one of promise." Paul combines Genesis 18:10 Genesis 18:14 from the LXX."[63] Paul makes this simple supporting connection here. "God appeared to Abraham, promising that He would return at the appointed **time** and that **Sarah** would **have a son**. That **son**, of course, was Isaac. He was truly a child of **promise** and a child of supernatural birth."[64] This supernatural aspect of Isaac's birth should not be passed over lightly. Not only was Isaac the second child born from Abraham, but also he was due only to God's supernatural intervention. Thus, we see a pattern that is developed in which God chooses the second, supernatural birth for His purposes and not the first natural birth due to human effort (works). Abraham and Sarah had to trust that God would fulfill His promise to bring a son through Sarah who was barren since the parents were incapable of achieving pregnancy on their own.

This second birth pattern is confirmed in the next verse where God again chooses the *second* child born. We will return to this topic again in the discussion on God's propose in sovereign choices (election) in a few verses. But here the thing to remember for this verse is that God makes His choice of Isaac as the line of Messiah in fulfillment of the *promise* He made to Abraham. *Promise* correlates to faith, as Law correlates to works. God returned to make good His *promise* through Sarah's pregnancy. God worked through Abraham and then Isaac establishing the Messianic line by His choice (election), not theirs (Abraham's or Isaac's).

10 And not only this; but when Rebecca also had conceived by one, even by our father Isaac;

Paul continues to follow the line of succession for the development of Israel and ultimately the line of Messiah. This expands on the statement in verse 5 where Paul summed up what God gave this privileged nation. Marvin Vincent summarizes the thought very well when he says:

> **And not only so,** The thought to be supplied is: Not only have we an example of the election of a son of Abraham by one woman, and a rejection of his son by another, but also of the election and rejection of the children of the same woman. **By one,** Though of one father, a different destiny was divinely appointed for each of the twins. Hence only the divine disposal constitutes the true and valid succession, and not the bodily descent.[65]

Thus, it was not due to having a different mother as in the case of Isaac, because Jacob and Esau had the same father and mother. It was due to God's choice (election) to fulfill His plan of redemption for the world. This is key to grasp at this point. Keep in mind that it is the second child born. The next verse will continue Paul's emphasis in this regard.

11 (For the children being not yet born, neither having done any good or evil, that the purpose of God according to election might stand, not of works, but of him that calleth;)

Most Bible translations add the parentheses on this verse (as in the KJV quoted above) because it is Paul's comment on the preceding verse. God made His choice (election) of Jacob before the children were born, which will be expounded on in the next verse. God made His choice of the second child prior to their birth, before either had the opportunity to do *good or evil*. Why did God do this? Paul answers—*that the purpose of God according to election might stand, not of works.* Indeed, God did not want human *works* involved in His redemptive plan. The salvation of man is never due to man's own efforts (*works*), but entirely due to the supernatural intervention of God. None of the normal, expected advantages of genealogy, being firstborn, or any other natural human advantage are used to establish the Messianic line and God's redemptive plan—only God's choice. The only thing natural about God's choices seem to be that they are contrary to naturally assigned human privileges.

We tend to think of *election* here as eternal life and nothing else. Typically, the frontloading of Calvinistic thought motivates this interpretation of the word *election* (no matter where it appears in Scripture). However, that would make the following verses very confusing, for it would declare that God elected certain people to eternal life and rejected others to eternal destruction for no apparent reason. Moreover, it would confuse the national context of Paul's teaching of Israel and connect *election* to an individual salvation of particular Jews (Isaac and Jacob). However, **the purpose of God according to election** is not that of individual eternal life and the logical opposite—eternal damnation! As Thomas Coke aptly comments:

> *Not as though the word of God had taken no effect,* or failed, &c. proving that God, according to his purpose of *election,* was free to confer them upon any branch of Abraham's seed. Consequently, those privileges were the singular blessings which, by the *purpose of God, according to election, not of works, but of him that calleth,* were conferred upon Jacob's posterity. But those privileges were only such as the whole body of the Israelites enjoyed in this world while they were the church and people of God, and such privileges as they might afterwards lose, or be deprived of; therefore the election of Jacob's posterity to those privileges was not absolute election to eternal life. ... the *purpose of God* according to election, it was said to Rebecca, *The elder shall serve the younger;* meaning, the posterity of the elder and the younger. For, Gen. 25:23 *the Lord said unto her, two* nations *are in thy womb, and two manner of* people *shall be separated from thy bowels; and the one* people *shall be stronger than the other* people, *and the elder shall serve the younger.* These are the words which signify the *purpose of God according to election.* Therefore the election refers to Jacob's posterity, or the whole nation of Israel; but the whole nation of Israel were not absolutely elected to eternal life... Therefore *the purpose according to election* refers to such privileges. The *election* here spoken of took place first in Abraham and his seed, before his seed were born; and then

(secluding Ishmael and all his posterity) in Isaac and his seed, before they were born; and then (secluding Esau and his posterity) in Jacob and his seed, before they were born. But the Scripture never represents *eternal life,* as bestowed upon any family or race of men in this manner.[66]

This second birth pattern is essential to understanding ***the purpose of God according to election*** and its connection to our text. What is God's purpose in ***election***? There are multiple aspects in God making choices (election) that become evident. First, there is the primary and redemptive purpose in fulfilling His covenant with Abraham. We see this in Genesis 12 and 15 where God created a nation to serve that purpose. Second, there is a secondary and principle purpose in the pattern of accepting only the second birth.

When we read the phrase "God's elect", it is not a mere statement of a fact or even of a purpose, but like the Scriptural expression "first born", it is a title of dignity and that title was only applied to those who were believers. The pre-eminent thought in Election is *rank and privilege,* not deliverance from damnation or eternal torment. This rank, this favor, this privilege, is shown to those people not before they are saved, but after. The word Election occurs 27 times in the Bible, and is used in connection with God's people.[67]

Finally, there is the natural result of these two aspects, which applies to the salvation of individuals. We will take a brief look at each.

The ***purpose*** in ***election*** fulfills God's word to Abraham as we have discussed, by making a nation from his offspring, providing a land for them, and the redemptive blessing for all nations. Paul has already introduced the fact that God used Israel and provided them the blessing of His word (divine revelation), with the benefits, education, and protection that accompanied it (Rom. 3:1-3, 31, 7:7, 9:4). It was necessary for God to make these choices, otherwise the salvation of man would have never occurred. God promised in the Garden of

Eden (Gen. 3:15) that He would send a Deliverer to solve the sin problem and conquer the devil. Thus, He was making good that promise by His covenant promise to Abraham. It was never left to man to invent or prescribe what was necessary for redemption; it was always God's job to solve the problem of man's need for redemption and to be the initiator of that plan. Moreover, He knew what He would do and how it would all work out from eternity past, before one atom of the creation was in existence.

Paul also introduced this pattern of God's choice to accept the second birth. Man is born the first time when he physically enters the world, but must be born again (John 3:3, 7), or literally, "born again from above" to receive eternal life. The second birth is the supernatural spiritual birth that only God through the Holy Spirit can perform (1 Cor. 12:13; Eph. 1:13; Titus 3:5). Man must believe (John 3:16), but in that act of faith God performs the supernatural work of redemption, resulting in justification (being placed in a righteous position before God). Paul introduced Abraham as the theological foundation for his teaching on justification (Rom. 4:1-4). This second birth teaching is parallel and inextricably connected to God's choice in His redemptive plan promised to Abraham. "Election is a divine act of God whereby God sets to one side all firsts and chooses all seconds. He sets to one side the first covenant in the Old Testament economy and chooses the second."[68] To bolster the point, God will also discard the first heaven and earth and create the second (Rev. 21:1). Additionally, we see in Paul's explanation of the resurrection in 1 Cor. 15:40-49, that the first body is changed into the second. In other words, the natural body (mortal) is changed to a spiritual body (immortal). The first Adam imparted physical life; the last Adam (Christ) imparted spiritual life. The point here is that there is again a principle of accepting the second, though it is numerically the same body in the resurrection, the first body is changed not replaced. In other words, Jesus body was changed not replaced, hence the empty tomb.When we believe in Jesus Christ and are born again

(John 3:16), we move from the race of Adam where we receive our physical life, to the new race in Christ where we receive our spiritual life. The principle seen in the pattern of the second in Scripture is too numerous to overlook as mere coincidence.

Finally, there is an aspect of individual salvation we see here as a natural byproduct of this second birth. Salvation is by faith in Jesus Christ alone (Rom. 5:1) and has no connection to the works of man (Rom. 3:27, 4:6, 9:11, 32, 11:6; Gal. 2:16, 3:10). This is why when Paul introduces this chapter with his heartfelt desire for the salvation of his ethnic kinsmen (Israelites), he enters into the discussion of the national benefits they received and how the nation itself was brought into existence—it was all the plan and program of God, in other words, all based on His choices (elective decisions).

The primary feature of God's elective *purpose* can be seen through the implementation of His redemptive plan, separating it from any human reliance for its accomplishment. God makes the choice of how man is redeemed, not man. Genesis chapter 4 tells of Cain, who tried to approach God based on his own methods, specifically ignoring God's instructions. The rebellious outcome was Cain's own frustration and the murder of his brother Abel. This is what happens when man tries to instruct God as to how he should be accepted for salvation—it's not pretty. God is the one that decides (elects) how His redemptive plan will occur and the requirement (faith) for acceptance. Paul shows both these aspects in this chapter. Therefore, God's *purpose* in election, or His *purpose* in the redemptive plan is to make sure all aspects of it are removed from the hands of man. Thus, no human merit, genius, works, schemes, planning or suggestion has anything to do with man's salvation. God initiates the entire plan from before the foundation of the world to the end of time. He has set one requirement for man to accept His choice in this regard, which is faith. Man's faith (trust) is sovereignly chosen by God as the requirement to receive His salvation. Paul hammers this subject home throughout the epistle of Romans. It is impossible to miss. Every chapter emphasizes that faith is the only condition God will accept. He develops his doctrine from the example of Abraham used earlier in the epistle, which he bases on Genesis 15:6, and follows it through to our current chapter. There is no theme separation regarding faith in the Bible or in this epistle. This subject is consistent and foundational to everything Paul—and the Bible— teaches.

Some commentators try to interpret one of these three points to the exclusion of the others, but it is unnecessary. Each one is part of the teaching of Paul, and as we will see in the verses that follow, God not only had a plan for Israel but for the world. Aside from teaching that this chapter is a limitation of salvation to certain individuals (according to Calvinistic theology), it actually teaches the opposite. Paul shows how the gospel is available to the entire world, and the only criterion on man's part to receive it is faith in Jesus Christ. Therefore, opposed to a limitation, it is an extension of the gospel to the whole world.

12 *It was said unto her, The elder shall serve the younger.*

This quote, *it was said unto her,* is from Gen. 25:23. Rebecca was having a difficult pregnancy and sought the Lord as to why. The answer was, "...the LORD *said unto her*, Two nations are in thy womb, and two manner of people shall be separated from thy bowels; and the one people shall be stronger than the other people; and the elder shall serve the younger." Notice, the answer the Lord gave was that there were two nations in Rebecca's womb. Thus, God foresaw the beginning of a battle of nations in this young girl's womb, not the salvation of the individuals. This was not lost on Paul and he was very aware of the context of the verse to which he referred. This is in line with the redemptive program worked through Abraham for the blessing of the world. The focus is now moved from Isaac to Jacob.

Esau was born first, but did not receive firstborn status in his family or with God. Similar to Ishmael who was born first, he also did not receive firstborn status. Firstborn is a term that relates to the priority given, or the preeminent position by the term firstborn. Indeed this is fitting because Jesus Christ is the firstborn (Col. 1:15), and it solidifies the connection with the genealogy chosen to bring about His physical birth. Being born first is not always equal to firstborn. When the term firstborn is used theologically, it refers to the priority, preeminence or favored status regarding position. It can refer to the one born first; however, the context establishes its usage. Since Jacob received this favored position, Esau became subservient to him and God made sure that Israel (Jacob's offspring) was *served* by Esau's offspring (Edomites). This was a national call on Esau's life and not related in any way to the individual salvation of either child. It was a call to service; the verse makes that abundantly clear. "The purpose of Election then, is that the first shall become subservient and serve the second."[69] The following verse gives the future history of the nations fathered from these children and reveals the preeminent position of Israel, contrasted with the judgment of Edom.

13 *As it is written, Jacob have I loved, but Esau have I hated.*

Bible commentators are divided as to whether or not Paul is speaking of individuals in these verses or nations; the answer is both. Jacob received the benefit of God's protection because of the nation that was to come from him (his twelve sons fathering the twelve tribes), and God confirmed the Abrahamic covenant with him in Gen. 28:13-15. Esau did not receive the same level of care that Jacob did since Esau's offspring was not the Messianic line and thus not afforded the same privileges.

The care and privilege here is expressed in the term *loved*. It is a term of decision supported by the context that Paul quotes from Malachi. God speaks through the prophet to Israel and says, "I have loved you, saith the LORD. Yet ye say, Wherein hast thou loved us? Was not Esau Jacob's brother? saith the LORD: yet I loved Jacob, And I hated Esau, and laid his mountains and his heritage waste for the dragons of the wilderness" (Malachi 1:2, 3). Malachi was the last to prophesy in the OT about 400 BC, after Israel returned to their land from the Babylonian captivity. Israel was facing the same problem that both Ezra (Ezra 9) and Nehemiah (Neh. 13) had previously addressed. God appealed to the nation that His treatment of them was one of *love* and care. He said, "I have loved you, saith the LORD" because they enjoyed favored status as the promised and protected nation bearing the Messianic line. In their spiritual dullness, they respond with "Wherein hast thou loved us?" the answer is what we read in Romans 9:13. Thus, when Malachi prophesied, Jacob and Esau were long gone and only the resulting nations were in existence. The individual children are mentioned because they are the source of those nations, but within the development of the nations, only Jacobs's offspring was under God's special care of *love* because of His covenant with Abraham. Indeed, *love* is not the emotional aspect we often associate with it (though that can certainly be part of it), but here it is the decision to fulfill the promise made to Abraham. It is a term of comparison such as "love less," but it is also a term of loyalty. Loyalty in relation to *love* is certainly a lost concept in our current culture, which is why we cannot properly interpret the Bible if we read the twenty-first century culture back into it. This is not a Hollywood love story drama; this is God working through history managing the nation He created from Abraham to bring the Savior into the world. To accomplish that end, Israel was given (and still has) a unique relationship to God as a nation. Paul in Romans 11 further develops this aspect of God's relation to national Israel.

The Bible defines and measures love differently than our secular culture does. This can certainly cause confusion when reading the Bible; therefore, our definitions must be taken from the Bible and not from the culture. Jesus said, "If any man come to me, and hate not his father, and mother, and wife, and children, and brethren, and sisters, yea, and his own life also, he cannot be my disciple" (Luke 14:26). All disciples are believers, but not all believers are disciples. To become a "born again" believer, faith alone is required. To be a disciple of Jesus Christ, there must be devotion and loyalty beyond our initial faith for salvation. This loyalty would in fact make all other relationships look like "hate" in comparison. Certainly, Jesus is not telling people to hate their closest family relationships. He wants us to love our enemies (Matt. 5:44; Luke 6:27), why would He want us to hate our family? Naturally, and especially in the context of first century Israel, loyalty would be the strongest in family relationships. However, if God is not first in our lives, no other relationship—including family—will have true *love* expressed. Our best option for treating our families in the way that they benefit most in this life is to have our first and most precious loyalty to Jesus Christ. It was due to God's commitment to His promise to Abraham that He advanced the nation of Israel in its call, and all nations received the ultimate benefit in the birth of our Lord and Savior Jesus Christ into the world.

Finally, before we leave this verse it is important to note that when Calvinists make the claim that God made an unconditional decision in eternity past to *love* and save *Jacob*, and *hate* and eternally condemn *Esau*, they create a biblical conflict. First, Calvinists teach that God eternally condemned *Esau* for no apparent reason before creation (the doctrine of reprobation). Calvinists call this election of one person to salvation and another to hell "double predestination." This doctrine is not found in Scripture, but is the logical conclusion resulting from Unconditional Election. If God elected *Jacob* before his birth, then He also condemned *Esau* at the same time to an eternity in hell by not electing him to heaven. This is the only conclusion available in Calvinistic theology, but it is not anywhere in the text! Hell was "prepared for the devil and his angels" Jesus said (Matt. 25:41). The implication is that it is a place for those who rebel (like the devil and his angels) against God, not those who God previously determined would be there from before the foundation of the world. It is the answer to the initial rebellion by the devil, the only place of eternal consignment or quarantine since heaven is the destination of those who exercise faith in Jesus Christ and love God. It is not the result of God determining who will go there before they actually rebel against Him in time. God knows who will rebel, but knowing is not determining. Hell is the necessary consequence of those who rebel against God. Therefore, isolating the verse with no respect or reference to other Bible passages that deal with the subject puts Calvinism in conflict with the Bible.

Second, since Paul is quoting Malachi at the time when both Israel and Edom were developed nations, there is a reason for God to *hate* the Edomites. The minor prophet Obadiah expresses the judgment upon Edom for their terrible treatment of Israel. God's *love* was expressed in Israel as God kept His covenant with Abraham and preserved them to fulfill His plan through them. God *hated* Edom which was seen in His act of judgment against them for their judgment against Israel—whom God was defending, preserving, and working His purpose through to bring about the redemptive blessing to the world. Thus, there is a reason for God to exercise His *hatred* (judgment) against Edom. This has no connection with decisions made before the foundation of the world for the individual salvation of Jacob and Esau. If Calvinists impose their unconditional election on this verse, without realizing it they take a "conditional" situation in history and change it to an "unconditional" decision made by God from before the foundation of the world. You cannot have it both ways. Therefore, Calvinists put themselves in logical, historical, and theological conflict with themselves, history, and the Bible.

14 *What shall we say then? Is there unrighteousness with God? God forbid.*

Paul anticipates this question as an objector would challenge, though no actual objector (interlocutor) is challenging him. This is a literary device for answering a question anticipated in the minds of the recipients of the letter. Is God unrighteous because He made the choice to create the nation of Israel, bless, and protect them to bring about His redemptive plan for the world?

God forbid (strongest term in Greek for *absolutely, positively not!*). God must make choices, otherwise the redemptive program and salvation of man would never take place. In order for man to have the opportunity to respond, God must first initiate as I have discussed. Once again, Paul will back up his claim with Scripture.

Imagine the attitude of a child growing up with all the privileges and benefits of loving parents, a stable family, secure home, and never wanting for anything, all while at the same time watching friends and others struggle to make ends meet. The child enjoys these privileges while growing up, respecting the parent's decisions because of the love and benefits conferred, though not necessarily understood or appreciated. When a young adult, circumstances in the family status change and the parent's decisions had to change with it. What had been enjoyed as normal benefits in younger years changed with the new circumstances, and the child was asked to trust the parents. The grown child is unaware of all the reasons for the change in circumstances, but they have their suspicions. After receiving a life of love and care, the parents assume their child will trust them based on a history of love and care. However, as age brings more knowledge about the world, the now young adult thinks they know more than the parents. Throwing off the parents' yoke, the child forgets their heritage, ignores their family relationship, rebels, and goes off to their own way. This is an all too familiar story in our culture, and in this type of discouraging family circumstance parents ask themselves many searching questions. Did their children learn anything over the years? Are they not able to understand the past was preparation for the future? Did they not recognize their parents' loving sacrifice and devotion to them? etc. etc...

Here we have Israel like a privileged child in comparison to the rest of the world, now thinking they know better and can do better for themselves rather than listen to the God who lovingly and patently reared them as a nation. Israel watched other nations fall into destruction and judgment because of their very treatment of Israel—God's people (the pre-exilic Minor Prophets especially reveal these judgments). Israel loved and enjoyed all the benefits (Rom. 9:6), but now because the gospel is preached to the Gentiles (Acts 22:21-22), they now question God's decisions, reject His plan (that was anticipated prophetically) and claim a moral infraction upon God. Paul's answer to this imaginary "Jewish" objector is brilliant.

15 For he saith to Moses, I will have mercy on whom I will have mercy, and I will have compassion on whom I will have compassion.

This is a quote from Exodus 33:19. Remember, the biggest mistake people make when reading the NT is ignoring the context of quoted passages from the OT. So let us look at the context, which we know Paul knew very well.

Back in the Exodus context and prior to the verse quoted, Israel had rebelled against God in the golden calf incident (Exodus 32) while Moses was on the mountain receiving revelation from God. God told Moses to go down from the mountain because the people had corrupted themselves (Exodus 32:7). They were a stiff-necked people (32:9) and God offered to destroy the nation and start over with Moses (32:10). Moses then interceded for the rebels, appealing to God's covenant with Abraham, Isaac, and Israel (Jacob) (32:11-14). God then relented of the initial course to destroy them (so much for determinism).

When Moses descended the mountain he dealt directly with the golden calf incident. At his invitation, his own tribe of Levi came together with him to destroy the rebels, and "three thousand men" died in judgement that day (32:15-29). The next day Moses told the people they "committed a great sin," but he would appeal to God to see if atonement could be made for them. He then made intercession for them. However, God let Moses know that punishment was coming to those who sinned against Him because of the idolatry of calf worship (32:30-35). Indeed, we have two parallel activities going on here. On the one hand, God promises to keep His covenant with Abraham by offering Moses the opportunity to be the patriarch of a new

Israel. On the other hand, we see the judgment of God against an idolatrous and stiff-necked people for their rejection of Jehovah and violation of the law they just agreed to keep.

Exodus 33 continues the event. God instructs Moses to continue on to the Promised Land and that He would give the guidance of His angel, but He would not be among them because of the sin. His presence among them could cause them to be consumed because they are a "stiff-necked people." When the people heard this, it resulted in a great mourning among them (33:1-6). Moses then made a temporary tabernacle separated from the camp which enabled a separation between himself and the nation (33:7-11). Then Moses appealed to God for His presence to go with them (33:12-16). This was something that Moses was accustomed to because God spoke "face to face" (33:11) with him and he experienced God's presence in the "cloud" (Exodus 19:9, 24:16, 18). Finally, God granted Moses' request because Moses found grace in God's sight (33:17).

Verse 17 (often overlooked), is a key verse in comprehending the context of the Exodus passage, it is essential to understand it properly. Typically, verse 19 is the only area of focus because it is the one Paul quotes. Indeed, the obvious question at this point is why did Moses find grace in God's sight? The answer in the context of the passage is clear; God judged those who rebelled (32:33), even though Moses appealed to God on their behalf (32:30-35). Then God instructed Moses to "Depart, and go up hence, thou and the people which thou hast brought up out of the land of Egypt, unto the land which I sware unto Abraham, to Isaac, and to Jacob, saying, Unto thy seed will I give it" (33:1). God not only renews the covenant at this point, but also makes it clear that the actions He takes are in support of that very purpose. Moses is an integral piece of God's purpose in moving the Abrahamic covenant forward along with the covenant of the Law; thus God preserves Moses through these events. Important to note is that God is gracious to Moses because of Moses' faith in God. Moses was a sinner no different than every other human, but God makes it clear in His relationship with man that humble faith is the basis of man's relationship with Him. Pharaoh did not humble himself (Exodus 10:3) and incurred God's judgment, though God was patient with him throughout the judgment of the ten plagues. At any point during the plagues, Pharaoh had the opportunity to respond to God in faith, but never did.

God is here acting on His promise to Abraham (Genesis 3:15) to bring the Savior into the world. Similarly and previously, we see God extended grace to Noah (Genesis 6:8) because it says, "Noah was a just man and perfect in his generations, and Noah walked with God...with thee will I establish my covenant" (Genesis 6:9, 18). Moreover, God does not only extend His grace to those who are integral in moving His purposes forward like Noah and Moses, He extends grace to all who will humble themselves before Him. "Surely He scorns the scornful, But gives grace to the humble" (Prov. 3:34, NKJV). In the NT, both James and Peter continue this theme: "But he giveth more grace. Wherefore he saith, God resisteth the proud, but giveth grace unto the humble" (James 4:6), and "God resisteth the proud, and giveth grace to the humble" (1 Peter 5:5). Their admonitions follow their statements, "Humble yourselves in the sight of the Lord, and he shall lift you up." (James 4:10), and "Humble yourselves therefore under the mighty hand of God, that he may exalt you in due time" (1 Peter 5:6). These verses make it plain that God responds graciously to man's humble faith. Responding to God's grace by faith is what being humble before God is about. If God did not initiate by grace in the first place, man would have no opportunity to respond. "For the grace of God that bringeth salvation hath appeared to all men, Teaching us that, denying ungodliness and worldly lusts, we should live soberly, righteously, and godly, in this present world" (Titus 2:11, 12). It is the grace of God that man has anything offered to him at all, as Whedon so aptly comments on in this extended quote:

> God thus willed, in spite of Moses' wish, to punish the guilty, and THE GUILTY ONLY; and he willed, in accordance with Moses' wish, to show him his glory. Thus did God will as he was supremely pleased to will. Yet let four things be

noted: First, this willing as he will does not mean willing without a reason, motive, or rule, but willing with a perfect right, reason, motive, and rule. Second. It does not mean that the reason, motive, or rule is an incomprehensible, mysterious, unrevealed, unknown one, but the fully revealed and perfectly just rule of impartially dealing with men as free agents. Third. The peremptoriness of this willing as he will, while it does not exclude either reason, rule, or a publication of reason or rule, does override the small caprice of the man who (as Moses) would doubt, cavil, or rebel against the infinite reason; and, Fourth, This willing as he will is a willing to deal with men, not "for nothing in them," but according to their faith, and subsequently to their faith, and conditionally upon their faith. The wrongly praying Moses is the type of the weeping Paul, or even of the cavilling Jew, humanely wishing that God would spare the unfaithful people; yet God will inflexibly act on the known and universally published rules of righteous judgment. He will disregard human dictation, whether in form of prayer, weeping, or cavil, and so will have mercy on whom he will have mercy. And human reason, being finitely in the type of divine reason, when it comes to an understanding of the divine rules and reasons, does in its highest exertions profoundly approve the principles on which they are based. So that Paul's logic is a full reply to his Jewish opponent.

In this interpretation we make no mistake. We have rightly interpreted God's words to Moses as they are in the Old Testament. And on the perfectly just rule that, where possible, a quotation in the New from the Old Testament must be taken in its original sense, the passage means from the pen of Paul just what it means from the mouth of Jehovah.[70]

Therefore, as we look at Exodus 33:19 (the verse in question), we see that Moses appeals to God to show him His glory (33:18), but it is based on the previous statements that Moses found grace in God's sight (33:12, 17). There was no mercy for the idolaters that rebelled (32:33), but there was for Moses who humbly appealed to God in response to His word, concluding simply that God extends grace to the humble and resists the proud. The humble do not *earn* God's grace, but they *receive* it by faith.

Paul undoubtedly realized what had transpired between God and Moses. He obviously felt in some sense that as Moses was desirous that Israel believe and walk with God; Paul desired the same (Rom. 9:2-3). What's important to note here is that the nation of Israel is under discussion in both Exodus and Romans. Showing mercy was not limited to the individual as Calvinists tend to interpret, but the context clearly favors the nation of Israel with the privileges and benefits God bestowed to them. God's **mercy** is exercised in accordance with His will in His **purpose according to election**, which is to advance His redemptive plan and offer salvation to those who will believe. The broader body of Israel was opposed to the plan of God in the gospel of Jesus Christ. Thus, with Israel's unwillingness to repent and believe the gospel, they were removing themselves from God's mercy, but only temporarily (Rom. 11:25). For as Paul will go on to say in chapters 10 and 11, God's plan for Israel ultimately is not changed, it is only deferred.

God makes it clear to Moses that He makes the decision as to whom He is merciful and to whom He is gracious. As we see in the Exodus passage, those who are not resisting His will receive mercy. But what is His will? It is to fulfill the covenant made to Abraham, reaffirmed to both Isaac and Jacob, that Israel be brought into the Promised Land, and through that nation, both the word of God and Messiah of God will come to the world. Though God can and does exercise His sovereign will, it is not arbitrary or entirely unknowable as to the conditions of showing mercy. Even the king of Nineveh—a wicked pagan —knew that humbling himself and his people before God held out the possibility for mercy (Jonah 3). The king of Nineveh realized that if God just wanted to immediately destroy the

Assyrians, the announcement by Jonah was unnecessary. The announcement of judgment is the opportunity for repentance and faith. Whether the judgment arrives immediately or is delayed is the decision of God, and that decision is at times based on the response of those on whom the judgment is announced. Part of Israel's problem was they actually thought that all Jews were by their genealogical association to Abraham accepted by God. But faith is the key to relationship with God and He extends mercy to those who will believe, as Whedon comments:

> **"I will... on whom I will**—This simple assertion, that God will accept whom he pleases, decides not the question, Whom does he please or will to accept? But, taken in its connections, it plainly means that whereas the Jew wills that God should accept all Jews, God wills—and **will** do as he wills—to accept all true believers. Paul thus peremptorily asserts not the divine **Will** in disregard of reason, or in disregard of "anything in the individual," or in regard to some unknown reason, or in absolute "divine sovereignty" over all things, but in entire independence of Jewish pedigree, merit, or dictation. The Jew prefers a system of predestinated birth-salvation; God prefers an equalized system of free-agency—and **will** have his way. He **will** have his way in spite of the cavils of predestinarians, whether Judaistic or Calvinistic.
>
> The rules by which God thus wills, and absolutely pleases, to have mercy, are abundantly revealed in Scripture. To reveal and publish them is, indeed, the great object of Scripture. The decalogue proclaims him a God "showing mercy to thousands that love me and keep my commandments." "Let the wicked forsake his way, and return to the Lord, and he will have mercy. (Isa. 55:7.) The pretence, therefore, that this verse presupposes some no-reason, or some unknowable reason, for his gracious preferences, is a figment and a folly."[71]

Paul sets up the verses to follow, for as Israel in the OT resisted God's purpose and did not believe, Israel during Paul's day rejected God's purpose when He revealed Jesus of Nazareth as the Messiah, as they continue to do today.

16 *So then it is not of him that willeth, nor of him that runneth, but of God that sheweth mercy.*

This verse has suffered a lot of contention between Calvinists and non-Calvinists. There is a lack of objectivity at times even among non-Calvinists. William MacDonald provides us a fitting comment on this verse that touches the heart of the matter:

> When Paul says that **it is not of him who wills**, he does not mean that a person's will is not involved in his salvation. The gospel invitation is clearly directed to a person's will, as shown in Rev. 22:17: "Whoever desires, let him take the water of life freely." Jesus exposed the unbelieving Jews as being unwilling to come to Him (John 5:40). When Paul says, **nor of him who runs**, he does not deny that we must strive to enter the narrow gate (Luke 13:24). A certain amount of spiritual earnestness and willingness are necessary. But man's will and man's running are not the primary, determining factors: salvation is of the Lord. [G. Campbell] Morgan says:
>
> > No willing on our part, no running on our own, can procure for us the salvation we need, or enable us to enter into the blessings it provides. ... Of ourselves we shall have no will for salvation, and shall make no effort toward it. Everything of human salvation begins in God.[72]

Vincent says of the grammar, "**It is not of him that willeth nor of him that runneth.** *It*, the participation in God's mercy. *Of* him, i.e., *dependent upon*. *Runneth*, denoting strenuous effort. The metaphor from the foot-race is a favorite one with Paul. God is laid under no obligation by a human *will* or a human *work*."[73] No matter who it is, God's *mercy* is always shown to those who align themselves with His redemptive plan, not those opposed to it.

> For Abraham judged that the blessing ought, and desired it might be given to his eldest son Ishmael; and Isaac

also designed it for first-born Esau: and Esau, wishing and hoping it would be his, readily went a hunting for venison, that he might receive it. But they were all frustrated; Abraham and Isaac who *willed,* and Esau who *ran;* for the blessing of being *a great nation,* and his peculiar people, God, of his mere good pleasure, originally intended first for Isaac, and then for Jacob and his posterity; and to them it was given. And when by their apostasy they had forfeited this privilege, it was not Moses's *willing,* nor any prior obligation that God was under, but his own sovereign mercy, which continued the enjoyment of it."[74]

However, it must be noted that God's *mercy* aligns with His plan, so it is no mystery as to His reason to show *mercy*.

This verse has one more word that deserves our attention. What is the *it* Paul refers to in the verse? He refers to God showing *mercy*. Certainly, God is the one that decides who He will and will not show mercy towards, but is His reason for doing so arbitrary or unknowable? Indeed, this is the question! The answer is it is knowable because as referenced in the comments on the previous verse, God shows *mercy* to the humble. In this context, He is not referring to the *mercy* to elect certain individuals to salvation. This would be an alien concept imposed on the text. He is referring to the working out of His overall plan of redemption through the nation of Israel. It is not human *will* or human effort (*runneth*) that accomplishes His plan, but God showing *mercy* to those who willingly align with His work and humbly receive it by faith. God can provide *mercy* to or hold it back from whomever He *wills*, but it is not arbitrary or haphazardly done. It is in accordance with His plan revealed in Scripture, of which Abraham, Isaac, and Jacob are an integral part. Yes, He chose to use them and the nation He developed from them, but His choice of them was His own and not theirs—not their *wills*. The success of that plan was because of God showing *mercy* to those along the way that did not deserve it, but had He not, there would have been no nation to bring the Messiah into the world. Considering His perfect record of accomplishment, no doubt God will continue to sovereignly accomplish His plan initially revealed and promised to Abraham (Genesis 12, 15). He must be sovereign in His ability to exercise *mercy* to bring about His redemptive plan; otherwise, it would fail because men fail. This is why it is *not of him that willeth, nor of him that runneth, but of God that sheweth mercy.* God's redemptive plan of salvation was dependent upon Him; it always was and still is.

17 For the scripture saith unto Pharaoh, Even for this same purpose have I raised thee up, that I might shew my power in thee, and that my name might be declared throughout all the earth.

Giving us more detail about God sovereignly providing mercy to whom He wants to, Paul now brings up Pharaoh. Many people will resist God's plan, and Pharaoh was one of those people. Pharaoh is a great example because not only was he resisting God's plan to free Israel and further God's plan to the redemption of the world, but also Pharaoh had all the power of Egypt on his side that sets up a conspicuously dramatic historical scene. This created a showdown of competing powers—God and the gods of Egypt to whom Pharaoh relied on.

The quote in this verse is from Exodus 9:16; it is after the sixth plague of boils that broke out on both man and animal throughout Egypt (Exodus 9:9). "This plague was a direct affront to the sacred bull, Apis, of the god Ptah and the cow goddess Hathor."[75] All ten plagues were a public demonstration of God's power against the false gods worshipped in Egypt. God used judgment to reveal His glory and power to the Egyptians, and through Israel, to the world. Had Pharaoh not resisted Moses' demands to release Israel, there would be no contest to demonstrate or *show* His *power.*

The phrase *I raised thee up* is the Greek word exegeirō, and means "raised out, arouse, stirred, bring out of a state of indecisiveness." God could have destroyed Pharaoh immediately, or redeemed Israel when there was a different Pharaoh reigning, but He chose this Pharaoh. He did not choose him to go to an eternal ruin before the foundation of the world as Calvinists claim; that precondition must be imposed upon the text here and back in Exodus where the event occurred. What the text is telling us however is that God demonstrated His *purpose* through His great *power* in the deliverance of Israel out of Egypt, a nation that enjoyed the premiere status of being the most powerful nation at the time. This deliverance was prophesied to Abraham (Genesis 15:13-14). In addition, through this event God made His *name declared* (published) *throughout the earth* in contrast to the false gods worshipped by the Egyptians, and to whom they attributed their great power and success as a nation. There are multiple lessons in this for us, but here Paul makes the point that God shows mercy when it suits His redemptive plans and withholds it when it does not. History provides us the evidence that God was very successful in fulfilling His plan with Israel and making His *name declared throughout the earth*. Who has not heard of the Exodus story? As Godet aptly comments, "Even to the present day, wherever throughout the world Exodus is read, the divine intention is realized: "to show my power, and make known my name throughout all the earth."[76] Hence, the next verse.

18 Therefore hath he mercy on whom he will have mercy, and whom he will he hardeneth.

This context is within God's activity of His overall redemptive plan. With Abraham, Isaac, and Jacob He showed mercy, and initially He even did with Pharaoh. However, when Pharaoh would not yield to God's demands through Moses, Pharaoh exhausted God's mercy within the context of delivering Israel. God then judged Pharaoh while in the condition of the hardness of heart he developed. "Pharaoh repeatedly hardened his own heart, and after each of these times God additionally hardened Pharaoh's heart as a judgment upon him. The same sun that melts ice hardens clay. The same sun that bleaches cloth tans the skin. The same God who shows mercy to the brokenhearted also hardens the impenitent. Grace rejected is grace denied."[77]

Therefore, there is no unrighteousness with God because He has *mercy* on whom He wants to or *hardens* whom He wants—but not capriciously, arbitrarily or indiscriminately—there is a *purpose* in His acts. In verse 17, God said what His purpose is: "that my name may be proclaimed in all the earth" (NET). In verse 18, Paul expands on the example to show that God will be the one (not man) to exercise His *mercy* in such a way that His *purpose* will be accomplished. His name has been "proclaimed in all the earth" through the worldwide expansion of the gospel. The great commission even provides the application of it: "Go, therefore, and make disciples of all nations, baptizing them in the name of the Father and of the Son and of the Holy Spirit" (Matt. 28:19, HCSB). Notice, the baptismal formula is "in the *name* of the Father and of the Son and of the Holy Spirit." In Jesus' high priestly prayer recorded in John 17, four times Jesus referenced that He had both made known and used as protection God the Father's *name* to His disciples (John 17:6, 11, 12, 26). The power of this name was made known throughout the earth from the days of Pharaoh's attempt to thwart God in the OT, and now in the NT through the gospel of Jesus Christ to the world. Paul's focus is on the *expansion* of God's *name* in the world, not the *restriction* of it through Calvinistic limited atonement.

God is sovereign, and there is no one who will stand in His way to the accomplishing of His redemptive purpose—or any of His purposes. Moreover, there is nothing in this context or Paul's argument here that would require the infusion of God's unconditional selection of people for salvation or reprobation from the foundation of the world. Indeed, to impose it on the text changes the text to teach Calvinism, when that theology is not even within the purpose of Paul's argument. To subtly leaf it into the text changes it from Paul's teaching to Calvin's, and immediately derails the thought process of the apostle and distorts the meaning of the verses that follow.

19 Thou wilt say then unto me, Why doth he yet find fault? For who hath resisted his will?

Paul here assumes the response of the interlocutor (imaginary objector). The challenge is, if someone rebels against God, how can God fault them (like Pharaoh), since they are being used by God to further His plan? However, as demonstrated, *mercy* is available to all, but only those who resist it do it to their own destruction—i.e. they bring it upon themselves.

Paul's assumed objector at this point is unbelieving Jews which he correlates to Pharaoh. Thus, the perspective behind the objection is if Israel rejects God's current plan to work through the church (using Gentiles along with Jews) to forward His redemptive plan, why would God find fault with them, since their rejection moves His plan forward? This is very similar to the objectors' argument in Rom. 3:7 that says, "For if the truth of God hath more abounded through my lie unto his glory; why yet am I also judged as a sinner?" This question, like the current one, is aimed at removing responsibility and avoiding guilt. Romans 3:7 is in response to Paul's claim (Rom. 3:1-6) that if some Israelites did not believe the word of God which that nation kept, does that show that God is not faithful since they did not all believe? Of course not! God's faithfulness is demonstrated by His unchanging attitude toward man. If man sins, God judges him; if man repents, God forgives him. God is the consistent one and is faithful to His covenant promises. Indeed, it must be noted that the argument in Romans 3 would be unnecessary and invalid if man did not have libertarian free will. That very freedom allows one Israelite to believe and another to reject. Moreover, without that freedom, all of Paul's arguments are a waste of time, along with his heart-felt plea to his own nation since from a Calvinistic perspective, they are not all savable.

Paul here references a commonly misunderstood view of man's faith as it relates to God's faithfulness. Just because people do not believe the Bible does not mean it is not true, or that its words lack power. Nor does it mean God is not faithful in His covenant promises. Indeed, the fact that this argument is brought up by Paul here and in Romans 3 more than implies man's free will as mentioned, since a deterministic framework would render the issue Paul addresses here as meaningless. If determinism was the correct theological view of God's management of people, Paul is actually on the wrong side of the argument. For he assumes by providing the question the objector would ask, that those on the wrong side of the issue are those who think they cannot resist God's will. This is the objector's plea! If people believe or rebel at God's deterministic discretion, then asking any question about resistance to God's will makes no sense. Calvinists read the objection Paul addresses as if he is shutting down the objector by claiming, "God determines all things and you have to live with it." The objector then brings up the potter and clay next to bolster their position that man is clay and God is in complete control over the clay and either makes them believe or reprobates them. However, they avoid the reason Paul brings up the objector's position in the first place. Indeed, it is the Calvinists that always ask *who hath resisted his will?* as if doing anything contrary to God's will is impossible. Yet, Paul addresses the objector's challenge since it lacks validity because man can resist God by his will, just like Pharaoh. To assume differently can cause the misguided conclusion that unbelief in Israel means there is a problem with God's faithfulness or that His word lacks power. On the contrary, it is because of man's free will that he is personally responsible for resisting God. Yet if that enduring unbelief creates a hardened heart condition, God's using it to further His purposes is not equal to deterministically causing it.

20 Nay but, O man, who art thou that repliest against God? Shall the thing formed say to him that formed it, Why hast thou made me thus?

The potter and clay are familiar OT figures to which Israel was well acquainted with (Isaiah 29:16 – quoted here, 41:25, 64:8; Jer. 18:4, 6). Again, the interlocutor (objector) here is unbelieving Israel. They are the ones in the previous verse Paul answers, and here he assumes them in his response. It is important to note that in Jer. 18:1-11, God had Jeremiah go down to the potter's house and watch the potter working with the clay upon the wheel. God says something very interesting to Jeremiah. "O house of Israel, cannot I do with you as this potter? saith the LORD. Behold, as the clay is in the potter's hand, so are ye in mine hand, O house of Israel" (Jer. 18:6). This is a strong statement of God's sovereignty; He has absolute control over Israel as the potter does over the clay. Then God says something that is incredible! The sovereign God of the universe says,

> There are times, Jeremiah, when I threaten to uproot, tear down, and destroy a nation or kingdom. But if that nation I threatened stops doing wrong, I will cancel the destruction I intended to do to it. And there are times when I promise to build up and establish a nation or kingdom. But if that nation does what displeases me and does not obey me, then I will cancel the good I promised to do to it. (Jer. 18:7-10, NET)

God the Potter will adjust His treatment of nations based on their response to Him. This statement matches God's response to that of Nineveh in Jonah chapter 3. Not only so, but God then instructs Jeremiah:

> Now therefore go to, speak to the men of Judah, and to the inhabitants of Jerusalem, saying, Thus saith the LORD; Behold, I frame evil against you, and devise a device against you: return ye now every one from his evil way, and make your ways and your doings good. And they said, There is no hope: but we will walk after our own devices, and we will every one do the imagination of his evil heart. (Jer. 18:11-12)

This interchange between God and Israel is highly instructive regarding the Potter and clay. God is willing to change His decision to judge if Israel is willing to turn from their evil. The answer they give in verse 12 is very illuminating. They decide (not God) it is hopeless and want to continue to walk after their own sinful hearts and ways. The key to note in this passage is that God is not determinative; He is pleading with Israel through Jeremiah to turn from their wickedness. They refuse and say,

"We will do whatever we want to do! We will continue to behave wickedly and stubbornly!" (Jer. 18:12, NET). This answer is not in the text for literary enhancement to the story. It is there because they chose to stay hardened in their path of wickedness. If God determined what man meticulously does, again the passage makes no sense. In that case, it would put God in the position of making a disingenuous offer and man in the position of rejecting a choice they never had the opportunity to make since they could not choose otherwise. Imposing a Calvinistic theology on this passage distorts—at a minimum—God's nature and challenges the integrity of His character. If it is impossible for God to lie (Heb. 6:18), why is He (in a Calvinistic framework) lying to Israel and pretending to offer them something they have no choice to select? Indeed, this is the crux of the issue with determinism.

Israel knows that the Potter (God) has absolute sovereignty over the clay (Israel). Isaiah said:

> Woe to those who go to great lengths to hide their plans from the LORD. They do their works in darkness, and say, "Who sees us? Who knows us?" You have turned things around, as if the potter were the same as the clay. How can what is made say about its maker, "He didn't make me"? How can what is formed say about the one who formed it, "He doesn't understand what he's doing"? (29:15-16, HCSB)

This is the background for Paul's statement. In the Isaiah passage, Constable says of verse 15, "The political strategists seem to be particularly in view. They tried to hide their plans from the Lord so they could be their own masters, as they thought, to live as they pleased rather than as He instructed them. Previously King Ahaz had tried to hide his appeal to Assyria for help (ch. 7)."[78] Verse 16 is what Paul particularly refers to, Constable again says, "These politicians turned things upside down. They denied the Lord's distinctiveness, sovereignty, and wisdom - and attributed those characteristics to themselves (cf. Isa. 29:14; Isa. 45:9; Isa. 64:8; Gen. 2:7; Jer. 18:1-6; Rom. 1:25; Rom. 9:19-21). They told the Lord what to do rather than trying to discover what He wanted to do."[79] Thus, Isaiah makes a mockery of the idols and their makers, since the people that made them had power over their creations. How stupid to think the dumb idol would be their maker, when they made the dumb idol.

Considering this point in Paul's current context, Israel should submit to God's purpose and not question His plan. The comparison is between Israel and God; He is their Maker, which means that He created them for a purpose and has a plan for them. They have no power to change His purpose for them, in wisdom, they can only conform to His plan by faith. To attempt anything other than humble compliance would be a folly equal to the dumb idols and their maker. God benefitted Israel and they enjoyed His protection, provision, and promises until the gospel of Christ went to the Gentiles, and then they rebelled. Their self-righteousness motivated their rebellion, and now they question God's whole method and plan. They have come to think—as the Isaiah passage—that they are the decision makers and God is subject to their whims and wishes. They—like the wicked in Isaiah's day—have things backwards.

21 Hath not the potter power over the clay, of the same lump to make one vessel unto honour, and another unto dishonour?

Dr. Constable makes an important point regarding this verse:
> The illustration in this verse clarifies the inappropriateness of this critical attitude. Clearly Israel is in view as the vessel in the illustration (cf. Isa. 29:16; Jer. 18:6). Israel had no right to criticize God for shaping her for a particular purpose of His own choosing. Really Israel had nothing to complain about since God had formed her for an honorable use. Obviously the same is true of individuals.[80]

This illustration of Israel shows that God's plan for a person is honorable, not destructive no matter who they are. In the midst of looming judgment by Babylon, Israel was told by Jeremiah (29:11), "For I know what I have planned for you, says the LORD. I have plans to prosper you, not to harm you. I have plans to give you a future filled with hope" (NET). Regarding individuals, 2 Peter 3:9 tell us, God is "not willing that any should perish, but that all should come to repentance." Paul tells us in 2 Tim. 2:20-21, "But in a great house there are not only vessels of gold and silver, but also of wood and clay, some for honor and some for dishonor. Therefore if anyone cleanses himself from the latter, he will be a vessel for honor, sanctified and useful for the Master, prepared for every good work" (NKJV). Therefore, God has **power** (authority) over the **clay** to make it a **vessel** according to His plans. He desires to make it a **vessel** to honor, and if the clay is willing to "cleanse himself from the latter"—not like Israel in the Isaiah passage—they *can* be a **vessel unto honor**. Unfortunately, God's intention for man is not always within man's willingness to receive and humbly yield. Indeed, once again the passage would be meaningless and nonsensical apart from man's genuine freedom to choose one or the other option.

No one disputes the fact that a potter has power over the clay, which is why this verse and the whole passage is so interesting. As I mentioned earlier under the chapter Rediscovering Logic, epistemology is the study of how we know what we know, and ontology is the study of the nature of being (i.e. why things exist in the first place). Knowing this, we need to look at the argument Paul develops here. We can get lost in the epistemological aspect of his argument and debate the exact meaning of his interlocutor, but that does not answer the larger question. The issue at stake here regarding the debate over whether or not man has a free will should be evident. The ontological question is why Paul brings up any debate or argues for the righteousness of God in His acts if there is no free will in man in the first place. Indeed, if man has no free will, end of story! God did what He did and there is no reason to argue it since God deterministically made both the believers and unbelievers before they were born, so why argue for a case to defend the history of God's actions in time? Why attempt to convince believers that the challenge of unbelievers is baseless if they have no freedom to make real choices? The lack of freedom actually makes the interlocutor's case! Yet, Paul masterfully develops the argument from the OT and brings it right into the NT. According to Calvinists, unbelievers can never understand any of the OT or NT rebukes of their unbelief since they were born with such an inability that they can never make a libertarian free choice. If that is the case, why argue the point as if they should have made choices other than the choices they made? Indeed, the ontological question must be answered before we become trapped in the weeds of the epistemological morass. I have never known any Calvinist to answer the question without appealing to *mystery* or an artificially shortsighted explanation of God's sovereignty. As I also mentioned earlier, they (Calvinists) seem to know quite a bit about what is not knowable when it comes to these issues. However, if we read the Scriptures in a normal manner, the mystery is solved and God's nature and character as revealed in the Bible becomes immediately obvious.

22 What if God, willing to shew his wrath, and to make his power known, endured with much longsuffering the vessels of wrath fitted to destruction:

Paul now asks a question which spans the next few verses in the English Bible to make his point; it is a literary device typical of Paul (see examples; Rom. 3:3, 8:31; 1Cor. 12:29-30; 2 Cor. 3:1, 6:14-16; Gal. 1:10, 3:2-5). He again responds here to the interlocutor. The question extends through verse 24 and is straightforward. The first aspect of the question in verse 24 is the question as to whether God has the right to be *longsuffering* with those *fitted to destruction,* the obvious answer is of course He has that right! However, this does not mean God was determining their destruction apart from their free will rejection of Him. Nor is there any aspect of determinism within the emphasis of the question. The emphasis is on God's ability to reveal Himself through His *longsuffering* with those persisting in preparing *themselves* for His wrath. Paul is not teaching Calvinistic determinism. He has other things in mind which is clear from the overall context that is the exercise of God's own will to achieve His redemptive plan, while not violating the free will of those He ultimately saves or condemns. That ability is in keeping with what we know about His absolute sovereignty, omniscience, omnipotence, justice, mercy, love and grace.

Therefore, Paul's point is that Israel does not have to be a *vessel of wrath fitted to destruction*, Paul himself was not in that category and yet he was an Israelite. The verse does not say that it is God's will to deliberately prepare vessels for destruction; it says that God can *show His wrath and make His power known* by *enduring with longsuffering* those who resist Him. *The vessels fitted* (prepared) *to destruction* are resisting God's good intention for them against His will. Which as noted above, makes no sense to argue unless the resisters could have chosen otherwise. Paul applies this argument throughout this passage to the rebellious Jews, Whedon again aptly notes:

> Of these two vessels, the perverse vessel and the obedient vessel, Paul now unfolds, in less figurative phrase, the different treatment at the hand of God. Of the former vessel, the original representative instance still is the Jews of Jeremiah, (chapters 18, 19,) who persist in their perversity, and are again (Jer. 19:1) typified by Jeremiah as a broken potter's vessel, (passages which our readers should carefully study,) while their antitype is the unbelieving Jews of Paul's day, with a specimen of whom Paul is now reasoning. Of the latter or obedient vessel, the primitive type is naturally Jeremiah and the few faithful of his day; and their antitype is the us of Rom. 9:24, namely, Paul and his brother believers.[81]

Both God and man are involved in the process of whether or not man will be a *vessel of honor*. Assuming that man has a free will, this does not prohibit God's work in the life of that individual; we see this in the example of Pharaoh. God works to draw all men to Christ (John 12:32), but men also "love darkness" (John 3:19) and resist the work of God's Spirit (Gen. 6:3). Indeed, when it says that these *vessels* are *fitted to destruction*, Vincent insightfully explains it:

Not *fitted by God for destruction*, but in an adjectival sense, *ready, ripe* for destruction, the participle denoting a present state previously formed, but giving no hint of *how* it has been formed. An agency of some kind must be assumed. That the objects of final wrath had themselves a hand in the matter may be seen from 1Thess. 2:15, 1Thess. 2:16. That the hand of God is also operative may be inferred from the whole drift of the chapter.[82]

23 And that he might make known the riches of his glory on the vessels of mercy, which he had afore prepared unto glory,

This continues Paul's question, but he now swaps the focus to those who are saved—*the vessels of mercy*. Does not God have the right to **make known the riches of his glory** on the saved? On those who "are his workmanship, created in Christ Jesus unto good works, which God hath before ordained that we should walk in them" (Eph. 2:10)? Of course He has this right! These **vessels of mercy** are living in His will and glorifying Him by their faith in His Son, who is the focus and accomplisher of God's redemptive plan. As Godet says:

> By the words: *to make known the riches of His glory*, Paul alludes to the example of Moses, Rom. 9:15, who had asked God to *show him His glory*, exactly as by the expression of Rom. 9:22 he had reminded his readers of those relative to Pharaoh. These riches of glory are the manifestation of His mercy which heaps glory on the vessels of honor, as the manifestation of wrath brings down perdition on the vessels that are worthless. Glory is here particularly the splendor of divine love.[83]

Paul has been making the point that **vessels of mercy** are those who will humbly yield to the work of God and comply with His plan of redemption. God's **mercy** is surely made known through those who—though *deserving* judgement—receive His **mercy**. This is nothing new; we see God's **mercy** extended throughout the OT in multiple places. David for one discovered **mercy** in the adultery he committed with Bathsheba and the murder of her husband Uriah (2 Sam. 11,12). When he finally repented, he penned Psalm 32 and 51, but he discovered something about God's *mercy*. Psalm 32:10 says, "Many sorrows shall be to the wicked: but he that trusteth in the LORD, mercy shall compass him about." Jesus rebuked the Pharisees in Mark 9:13 because of their self-righteous, merciless attitude against sinners when He said, "But go and learn what this means: 'I desire mercy and not sacrifice.' For I did not come to call the righteous, but sinners, to repentance." This was an echo of Hosea's accusation against rebellious Israel, "For I desired mercy, and not sacrifice; and the knowledge of God more than burnt offerings" (Hosea 6:6). Additionally, who can forget Jonah and his frustration because God showed *mercy* to the Assyrians (Jonah 4:2) instead of judgment? This should not have dismayed Jonah since while in the great fish he expressed the condition of those to whom God shows his mercy, "Those who worship worthless idols forfeit the mercy that could be theirs" (Jonah 2:8, NET).

Indeed, *mercy* is available to those who humbly repent and receive the forgiveness and *mercy* that God desires to show to all (Rom. 11:32). Since everyone deserves judgment, any expression of *mercy* surely *makes known the riches of His glory*. God has a plan for everyone who will believe. As Paul wrote to the Ephesian church, "For we are his workmanship, having been created in Christ Jesus for good works that God prepared beforehand so we may do them" (Eph. 2:10, NET). Though God has a plan for those who will believe, unfortunately, many times believers do not walk in the plan that God has *prepared*. Though they may be saved, ultimately, they will receive nothing by way of reward (1 Cor. 3:15).

Paul now gets to where he was heading the whole time, God's redemptive plan intended for both Jews and Gentiles. He now completes the question in verse 24, drawing his conclusion.

24 Even us, whom he hath called, not of the Jews only, but also of the Gentiles?

Even us, who is Paul speaking of? *The Jews*, but he adds *but also of the Gentiles*—i.e. believers in Jesus Christ. How did they become so? By faith! They responded to the *call* (invitation) of God. God invites all and every *Jew* has the opportunity to believe. However "they are not all Israel, which are of Israel" (v. 6). All *Jews* knew God was looking for a response of faith by His promise regarding Isaac (v. 7)—which is contrary to coming to God based on good works (human effort and merit). Those that exercise faith in Christ are the ones God has *called* to Himself, the ones to whom He is making *known the riches of His glory*. These are the *vessels of mercy* mentioned in the previous verse. These are the ones who received the *mercy* of God, though they deserved judgment as sinners. God made known *the riches of His glory,* having *prepared* them for a future that God predestined. Man has no hand in the eternal redemptive plan of God; it is only by *grace* that man *is* saved, it is only by *mercy* that God *would* save.

However, someone had to pay the price! God would not be just if He turned His head from sin; He would have to deny His own nature of righteousness. He must redeem what man corrupted in His originally perfect creation. All wrongs must be righted if evil is to be judged and put away. That is where the Lord Jesus Christ comes in. He paid the price for our redemption by grace (we did not deserve it) and enabled the bestowal of God's *mercy* —showing *the riches of His glory*—on those who are *called* from both *Jews and Gentiles*.

God always had a plan to reach *Gentiles* with salvation. Paul makes that clear in the following verses. Should God be limited in His redemptive plan of salvation by the stubbornness of those in Israel who are displeased with it? No! Even Jesus made known to the Jews God's intention to reach Gentiles as Godet comments:

> And those predestined to glory, He has drawn by long-suffering, not only from the midst of the lost mass of the Jews, but also from among the Gentiles. This was what Jesus had declared: "I have yet other sheep which are not of this fold" (John 10:16). And this Paul had in view in the words: the riches of His glory. While He gleaned among

the Jews, He reaped a harvest among the Gentiles, and thus carried out, in spite of Jewish pretensions, the free and large plan of salvation which He had formed on the sole prevision of faith.[84]

In the election of the nation of Israel "the grace of God was not confined to the Jewish people, as they supposed, so that it could be conferred on no others."[85] Which is why Paul says *even us*, including himself (a Jew), but *also the Gentiles* through the redemptive program God planned before the foundation of the world (Eph. 1:4; 1 Pet. 1:20; Rev. 13:8).

Paul makes the argument in chapter 5 that Christ's sacrifice was to the whole world, which includes *Gentiles* and not *Jews* only. Coke makes the point when he says:

Here the Apostle advances his third and last argument, to prove the extensiveness of the divine grace, or that it reaches to all mankind as well as to the Jews. His argument stands thus: "The consequences of Christ's obedience extend as far as the consequences of Adam's disobedience; but those extend to all mankind; and therefore so do the consequences of Christ's obedience." Now if the Jews will not allow the Gentiles any interest in Abraham, as not being naturally descended from him, yet they must own that the Gentiles are the descendants of Adam, as well as themselves; and being all equally involved in the consequences of his sin, that is to say, temporal death and its concomitants, from which they shall all equally be released at the resurrection, through the free gift of God, respecting the obedience of Christ,—they could not deny the Gentiles a share in all the other blessings included in the same gift.[86]

It is clear that Paul continues his argument of the extent of God's offer of the gospel by grace to the world beyond the *Jews.* For he develops Israel's continued problematic relationship to the gospel in the following verses.

25 As he saith also in Osee [Hosea], I will call them my people,

which were not my people; and her beloved, which was not beloved.

William MacDonald has very instructive words on this verse when he says:

> The apostle quotes two verses from Hosea to show that the call of the Gentiles should not have come as a surprise to the Jews. The first is Hosea 2:23 : **"I will call them My people, who were not My people, and her beloved, who was not beloved."** Now actually in Hosea these words refer to Israel and not to the Gentiles. They look forward to the time when Israel will be restored as God's people and as His beloved. But when Paul quotes them here in Romans he applies them to the call of the Gentiles. What right does Paul have to make such a radical change? The answer is that the Holy Spirit who inspired the words in the first place has the right to reinterpret or reapply them later.[87]

Paul uses Hosea's quote to apply to the Gentiles because they received the gospel that Israel nationally rejected. Thus, those who received the gospel—God's *vessels of mercy*—are *called* His *people*. The fact that most of the church consists of Gentiles, instructs the Jews that God's redemption is not by ethnicity but by faith and extends to all who will believe. However, this also means that Paul identifies the unbelieving Jews as the *vessels of wrath* (v. 22). As Whedon says, "This presupposes the identity of the Church of Jesus with the spiritual side of the two lines above given, and the unbelieving Jews with the vessels of wrath, Rom. 9:22."[88]

Paul is building his case from the OT that the Jews should have been well aware that God was not only interested in the redemption of Jews. Thus, he continues to quote from Hosea to bolster his point.

26 And it shall come to pass, that in the place where it was said unto them, Ye are not my people; there shall they be called the children of the living God.

This quote is from Hosea 1:10. Originally the quote is in

reference to the future restoration of Israel. But here, as in the previous verse, Paul applies it to the Gentiles because they are the ones that have come to faith in Christ, answering to the redemptive plan of God for the world. Additionally, Paul eventually shows that the salvation of the Gentiles is part of the masterful means God employs to provoke Israel to jealousy for their restoration (Rom. 10:19, 11:11). Thus, Paul again applies this verse to the Gentiles in God's plan of the restoration of the Jews. Really, who could have dreamed up such a plan other than an omniscient God? He masterfully uses rebellion and unbelief to advance His purposes without violating man's free will. Discovering the brilliance of this plan should cause us to bow in worship and adoration to the God who is so wise in His planning and masterful in His implementation of it. Only the God revealed in Scripture can do this. He is sovereign and yet can allow man to exercise free will without hindering His redemptive plan for the world. Indeed, He uses the attempted hindrances to accomplish it when necessary.

Gentiles did not originally possess the natural benefits of the Jews (Rom. 9:4-5), since they were born outside of the nation of Israel. In reference to the Gentile's condition prior to the gospel of Jesus Christ, Paul said, "That at that time ye were without Christ, being aliens from the commonwealth of Israel, and strangers from the covenants of promise, having no hope, and without God in the world" (Eph. 2:12). This is a bleak picture indeed; however as MacDonald notes:

> In addition to being without the Messiah, the Gentiles were **aliens from the commonwealth of Israel**. An alien is one who does not "belong." He is a stranger and foreigner, without the rights and privileges of citizenship. As far as the community of **Israel** was concerned, the Gentiles were on the outside, looking in. And they were **strangers from the covenants of promise**. God had made **covenants** with the nation of Israel through such men as Abraham, Isaac, Jacob, Moses, David, and Solomon. These **covenants** promised blessings to the Jews. For all practical purposes,

the Gentiles were outside the pale. They were without **hope**, both nationally and individually.[89]

This was not a permanent condition; the promised Messiah to the nation of Israel would be available to the Gentile world through the gospel preached by the apostles (Acts 10:35, 13:26). It is because of that wonderful gospel of grace that Gentiles can now *be called the children of the living God.* Or, as Paul said, "But now in Christ Jesus you who once were far off have been brought near by the blood of Christ" (Eph. 2:13, NKJV).

Not only are Gentiles that repent and believe the gospel *called the children of the living God*, but "that the Gentiles should be fellow heirs, of the same body, and partakers of His promise in Christ through the gospel" (Eph. 3:6 NKJV). The point? "In other words, converted Gentiles now enjoy equal title and privileges with converted Jews."[90] There is no distinction in the Body of Christ, "For there is no distinction between Jew and Greek, for the same Lord over all is rich to all who call upon Him" (Rom. 10:12, NKJV). This lack of distinction in the church actually distinguishes the nation of Israel from the Body of Christ. The church does not replace Israel; it is a separate group with a separate eschatological future.

Paul does not quote Hosea chronologically, but uses the quotes according to *subject*, rather than the *sequence*. He follows this subject-oriented method in the following quotes from Isaiah.

27 Esaias also crieth concerning Israel, Though the number of the children of Israel be as the sand of the sea, a remnant shall be saved:

Here the quote is from Isaiah 10:22-23; the emphasis is that *Israel* certainly did not do anything worthy of God's blessing, but to the contrary, violated the Mosaic covenant. It was because of God's unconditional covenant with Abraham that God continued to exercise His own will to ensure the fulfillment of His plan of redemption. If it were up to the faithfulness of *Israel*, the plan would not have even got off the ground. This is

Paul's point, though *Israel* had grown to a large number, *as the sand of the sea* when Isaiah prophesied, only a *remnant* from that number would come to God by faith.

God knew (His omniscience) not all *Israel* would receive His plan of salvation, but that only a *remnant* would *be saved*. When we read there is a *remnant*, they were not *saved* by God's determination (as Calvinists would interpret). What should not be missed here is the context of the overall passage and Paul's particular focus. Paul places emphasis on the faithfulness of God to keep His covenant with Abraham and maintain at least a *remnant* of Jews who will come by faith. In just a few verses, Paul will tell us why the majority of *Israel* did not receive God's redemptive work through Christ.

Paul correlates the rebellion of the majority of *Israel* at the time of Isaiah, with the same unbelief Israel showed when Paul wrote. As Albert Barnes says:

Shall be saved - Shall be preserved or kept from destruction. As Isaiah had reference to the captivity of Babylon. This means that only a remnant should return to their native land. The great mass should be rejected and cast off. This was the case with the ten tribes, and also with many others who chose to remain in the land of their captivity The use which the apostle makes of it is this: In the history of the Jews, by the testimony of Isaiah, a large part of the Jews of that time were rejected, and cast off from being the special people of God. It is clear, therefore, that God has brought himself under no obligation to save *all* the descendants of Abraham. This case settles the principle. If God did it *then*, it was equally consistent for him to do it in the time of Paul, under the gospel. The conclusion, therefore, to which the apostle came, that it was the intention of God to reject and cast off the Jews as a people, was in strict accordance with their own history and the prophecies. It was still true that a remnant was to be saved, while the great mass of the people was rejected. The apostle is not to be understood here as affirming that the passage in Isaiah had reference to the gospel, but only that *it settled one great principle of the divine administration in regard to the Jews, and that their rejection under the gospel was strictly in accordance with that principle.*[91]

When Barnes (previous quote) says "God has brought himself under no obligation to save *all* the descendants of Abraham," he makes a key point and emphasizes the fact that God works by the principle of His own redemptive plan. In other words, He only saves those who come by faith. This is the theme throughout the chapter (and the Bible) and why Paul states early in his argument "they are not all Israel which are of Israel" (v. 6). Though God is under no obligation to save every individual Israelite, He is under obligation to fulfill His covenant with Abraham which He confirmed by an oath (cf. Heb. 6:16-18). However, regarding individual salvation, as recorded with Abraham (Gen. 15:6) it was always by faith. This includes the time Israel was under the Mosaic Law, and of course now that we are under grace. Therefore, God had every right to eliminate Israel because of their idolatry and wickedness (no evidence of faith), but promised to restore them because of His covenant with Abraham, which reveals His sovereignty, grace, and mercy.

28 For he will finish the work, and cut it short in righteousness: because a short work will the Lord make upon the earth.

Here Isaiah 10:23 is the reference. It is a bit different from the Hebrew OT since Paul quoted from the Greek Septuagint version (LXX) of the OT. "The apostle's words are nearly a verbatim quotation from the Septuagint, and so quite different from the English translation."[92] But the point is clear, if God allowed the work to extend indefinitely, no Jews would be saved. The corruption of the whole nation would eventually be the outcome and faith would be nonexistent. Therefore, in His sovereignty, God limited the time and determined to **cut it short**. What God did not do is limit the believers by Calvinistic determination. Paul broadens the scope from the Hebrew OT which reads "in the land" to the LXX which reads **upon the earth**.

Thomas Constable notes what becomes clear in the Hebrew quotation:

> God had promised Abraham that his descendants would be as numerous as the sand grains of the sea (Gen. 22:17; Gen. 32:12). This did not mean, as the Israelites in Isaiah's day apparently concluded, that they would always be a large people. No, God would so thoroughly destroy them because of their sin that only a small number would survive (cf. Rom. 9:27-28). The sovereign Yahweh of armies would destroy them throughout the whole Promised Land, not just in the Northern Kingdom.[93]

Thus, those in Isaiah's day would realize that the judgment coming would be severe, but not entire because of God's covenant with Abraham. The question is, why the enlarged scope of the *earth* (world) instead of limiting it to the "land" (Israel)? With the larger scope, God brought Gentiles into the redemptive plan along with Jews constituting the church of Jesus Christ. The people of God in the NT are not the nation of Israel as in the Old Covenant, but the church of Jesus Christ is under the New Covenant in His blood (Matt. 26:28).

The nation of Israel and the church of Jesus Christ are different in their composition and purpose. The nation of Israel contained both believers and unbelievers; the church contains only believers since you have to be born again (a regenerated believer) to be part of it (1 Cor. 12:13). Israel's purpose as a nation was to bring the word of God and Messiah of God into the world and be the vehicle through which God brings His Kingdom to the earth; the church is the Bride of the Messiah (2 Cor. 11:2), born from His work of redemption. Considering the Isaiah passage here, God's judgment on Israel was on the nation that contained both believing and unbelieving Israelites. But in the NT, the nation of Israel is separate from the church and contains what constitutes unbelieving Jews.

> Israel's election as a nation did not preclude God's judgment of the unbelievers in it. His mercy and faithfulness are observable in His sparing a remnant.

SCOTT MITCHELL

Isa. 10:22-23 anticipated the depletion of Israel through Sennacherib's invasion. That was God's instrument of judgment. When Paul wrote, the believing remnant of Israel was within the church, as it is today.[94]

Thus, Paul separates the two groups (Israel and the church) with his quote. He places the nation of Israel outside the believers of the church, since once a Jew becomes a believer in Christ they become part of the church. Moreover, within the church, a Jew actually loses their ethnic distinction relative to privilege in relationship with God. As Paul says, "For there is no distinction between Jew and Greek, for the same Lord over all is rich to all who call upon Him" (Rom. 10:12). Paul spells out this same truth in other places (Gal. 3:28; Col. 3:11). This ethnic connection is altogether different within the nation of Israel since it is ethnicity that defines the nation as such. Therefore, Paul uses this verse to emphasize that the current work of God in the world is through the Church of Jesus and not the nation of Israel. The change came with the change in covenant (Heb. 8:7-8, 13).

Eschatologically, God will once again turn His focus on Israel and work through them as the main vehicle to reach the world (subject of Romans 11), but this is only after the rapture takes place prior to the 7 year tribulation period. It is evident that the church is not in focus or even in the tribulation period. For Revelation chapter 7 divides the believers that are in the tribulation period into specific ethnic groups of Jews and Gentiles, when in the church there is no such distinction. Moreover, these particular Jews (144,000) in the tribulation are sealed (Rev. 7:3-4) for protection through that time, where the Gentile believers from all nations are not (Rev. 7:13-14). Creating this ethnic distinction among believers in the tribulation period cannot be the Body of Christ since that ethnic distinction and selective benefits to the Jewish believers (144,000) is different.

29 And as Esaias said before, Except the Lord of Sabaoth had left us a seed, we had been as Sodoma, and been made like unto Gomorrha.

Here Isaiah 1:9 is the reference. Paul's point here is very simple: unless *the Lord of Sabaoth* (armies) left some survivors, Israel would have been wiped out because of their sin just like *Sodom and Gomorrah*. When Isaiah made the statement, the nation was steeped in idolatry and wickedness. Isaiah chapter 1 gives a very bleak survey of the nation's spiritual condition: "From the sole of the foot even to the head, no spot is uninjured —wounds, welts, and festering sores not cleansed, bandaged, or soothed with oil" (Isaiah 1:6, HCSB). This is certainly not an enviable position before God. Therefore, the nation had nothing to brag about since their morality was no better than *Sodom and Gomorrah* in the sense that they persisted in wickedness, which in many cases was similar in their idolatrous worship—even after the warning of judgment. God said through Isaiah, "If you are willing and obedient, You shall eat the good of the land; But if you refuse and rebel, You shall be devoured by the sword"; For the mouth of the LORD has spoken" (Isaiah 1:19-20, NKJV). The last phrase emphasizes that judgment "by the sword"—a reference to the severe judgment of other nations—is unavoidable if there is no repentance. Paul shows that Israel does not have the great history of faith they may believe they did, when all the facts are observed. This is similar to Stephen's account of Israel's history before the Jewish leadership council in Acts 7. Specifically, Stephen gives the bottom line after his recounting of Israel's failure to receive its past deliverers and ultimately the Messiah when he says, "You stiff-necked and uncircumcised in heart and ears! You always resist the Holy Spirit; as your fathers did, so do you. Which of the prophets did your fathers not persecute? And they killed those who foretold the coming of the Just One, of whom you now have become the betrayers and murderers, who have received the law by the direction of angels and have not kept it" (Acts 7:51-53, NKJV). This is the same point Paul makes here with reference to the unbelieving Jews. Indeed, this is an interesting parallel since Paul was there when Stephen was stoned (Acts 7:58), and consented to it (Acts 8:1); therefore he must have heard

Stephen's defense before the ruling council. Paul was well-aware of what unbelief and hatred toward Jesus Christ felt like and looked like; thus he was most qualified to rebuke, admonish, and survey the nation's condition regarding their unbelief. He does it here with a broken heart (Rom. 9:1-3), and a keen understanding of how the OT Scriptures apply to their condition. "Grief for his unhappy countrymen filled the Apostle's heart: but, though the generality of them perished, the promise made to Abraham would not be frustrated."[95]

God knew that there would be fewer Jewish believers within the nation because of His foreknowledge. In its original context, this verse specifically relates to the number of Jews that would believe within the nation, a small percentage statistically. Paul applies the principle of the limited number of Jews who would come out of the nation to follow Jesus Christ. Certainly, this has been historically true looking back two thousand years, as it was in Paul's day. As we consider the number of Jewish believers even in the book of Acts, though large groups came to Christ (Acts 2:41, 4:4), this is a very small percentage within the nation. When we consider that the gospel is preached throughout the world, the percentage of Jews comparatively in the church has to be small. There are simply not enough Jews to create a large percentage of believers even if every Jew on the planet believed and were added to the number of Gentile believers. This simple mathematical analysis could have been easily anticipated if the OT quotes regarding the extension of salvation to the Gentiles (example: Isaiah 11:10, 42:6) through the Messiah was believed and considered.

The small percent of Jews that believe within the nation— OT or NT—is not a favorable comment of their faith in God. Paul was specific in quoting Isaiah to show that the Jews do not have a flattering history in this regard. He introduces this quote because he is going to inform the Jews (the next verses) that their perspective is misguided and what they think is faith is actually unbelief. The Gentiles have come to Christ in large numbers and have benefitted from their relationship with Jesus.

This has been a difficult pill for the nation of Israel to swallow since they have not received the same blessings and spiritual experiences. Paul eventually says that God will use His blessing on the Gentiles in the world in the development of the church of Jesus Christ as a method to stir a jealousy in the Jews to spark their faith (Rom. 11:11). Paul now concludes his presentation here in Romans 9.

30 What shall we say then? That the Gentiles, which followed not after righteousness, have attained to righteousness, even the righteousness which is of faith.

As Whedon remarks, this verse is:

...a reiteration of the first query of Rom. 9:14, introducing the final answer to the query of that verse. ...The Gentiles did not even pursue the game, and yet attained it; the Jews pursued, but, willfully and wickedly, in the wrong direction, and lost it. Yet, in a sense, the individual Gentiles who attained did seek by faith, though historically the mass of Gentiles had not sought.[96]

This could not be more clear; the Gentiles met God's demand for the requirement of faith. How tragic that the nation of Israel would not rise to this same place of faith. Whedon summarizes the chapter well:

Paul explicitly furnishes now the KEY, the secret of the Divine preference of a special Israel in Israel, (6-13,) of a mercy to Moses and a hardening upon Pharaoh, (14-23,) and, by special inference, of the prophesied reservation of a gracious remnant of fallen Judaism over the main mass, (24-29.) The key runs its solution through both columns of character given at our introduction to notes on 6-13. The entire secret is the faith-condition.[97]

What Whedon calls a "faith-condition" is a main theme running through the entire epistle. It is not so much a secret, unless you are trying to gain righteousness by works, in that case, it may indeed appear to be a secret.

31 But Israel, which followed after the law of righteousness, hath not attained to the law of righteousness.

Coke summarizes Paul's teaching on righteousness when he says,

> *Righteousness* or *justification*, is to be understood here, as Rom. 4:3,5. Gen. 15:6. It is the justification by faith, to which the Apostle from the beginning of the Epistle has been arguing and proving that the believing *Gentiles* have a right, and which they have attained; but which the unbelieving Jews have not *attained*, because they sought it not by faith, but by the works of the law, Rom. 9:32. Therefore what is meant by *attaining to this justification*, will be clearly understood, if we consider that the Apostle is here giving the reason why the Jews were cast off from being God's people, and the Gentiles admitted to that privilege.[98]

The term **law** here means principle; thus, Israel did not attain to **righteousness** as a principle of life, even though they pursued it. Their problem was (and is), that they assumed that merely possessing the law that God gave them made them righteous. They confused *possessing* the law with *attaining* **righteousness**. They had abided by these laws from the time of Moses, so they thought there would be no difference now in their condition for salvation. However, that would be the first mistake in their thinking, for salvation was always by faith, never by law - keeping. Paul clearly emphasized this earlier in the epistle (Rom. 4:13) as well as the epistle to the Galatians (Gal. 3:21). There is no law to follow that can redeem or give spiritual life (cf. Acts 13:39). The Mosaic Law was given for the sanctification of the nation of Israel, not their redemption. The gross misunderstanding of this fact has not only tripped up Jews, but also Gentiles who attempt to come to God by their own good works, no different than Cain (Gen. 4). This is why the nation did not attain righteousness, even though they tried to gain it by obeying the law. Indeed, Paul made the point in these verses that Israel did not even keep the law, but were as **Sodom and**

Gomorrah. Legal self-righteousness is always self-deceptive; it elevates the carnal nature of man and diminishes faith as a means of justification before God.

Some Christians try to mix the two (law and faith) without success; they always fall to the side of the self-righteous legalist and erode their spiritual condition and diminish their relationship with God. Our sinful nature—like Cain's—would love to have a hand in our salvation and take pride in our standing before God, but it is a work of God's grace and this is why God makes faith the condition for justification. Anything added to faith is deceptive and leads us to think we did something to save ourselves. Faith has no merit in it because it is not a work, it is a belief (Rom. 3:27); it is not a work of the hands, but trust in the heart (Rom. 10:9). Paul always contrasts law and grace, works and faith; he never confuses or combines them. Calvinists tend to conflate faith and works, saying that if a person exercises their own faith, somehow that is identified and defined as a work. No matter what kind of theological sleight of hand is used, this simply flies in the face of what the Bible clearly states. The requirement that God established for man to receive salvation by faith was not a requirement God made for Himself, but for man to exercise freely. It makes no sense to set a requirement that God would make for Himself—making people believe through Irresistible Grace—and then hold guilty those who do not exercise faith because He has not made them believe. This is the logical and theological contradiction within the Calvinistic framework, and no measure of explanation can remove the dilemma. Paul now gives us the reason Israel failed in their faith.

32 Wherefore? Because they sought it not by faith, but as it were by the works of the law. For they stumbled at that stumblingstone;

"**Wherefore**? - This *wherefore* really asks what was the solution of the election and rejection of Rom. 9:6-19, and the answer furnishes the solution. Reprobation is not antecedent to but consequent upon want of faith."[99] Whedon is entirely correct; reprobation is not "antecedent to" or before faith, but is "consequent upon" or resulting from a lack of faith. This eliminates the Calvinistic determinism that pictures God reprobating people prior to their birth. Indeed, if Calvinism were correct, the whole argument and purpose of Paul's argument and detailed points here in Romans 9 are senseless (which I have tried to point out repeatedly).

Paul actually concludes his overall argument on the subject of *faith* as a requirement for, and application to justification that he has established throughout the epistle. Ultimately, he must discuss the application of *faith* in the context of the chapters on Israel (9-11) so that it correlates to his doctrinal development of it in the previous chapters. Thus, he now gives us the bottom-line. Israel **stumbled** over the simplicity of *faith* in Christ. He became an obstacle to them; He got in the way of their system of works righteousness.

> The figure of *stumbling* is in keeping with all those that precede: *follow after, attain to, reach* (obtain). In their foolish course, Israel thought they were advancing on a clear path, and lo! all at once there was found on this way an obstacle upon which they were broken. And this obstacle was the very Messiah whom they had so long invoked in all their prayers! But even this result was foretold.[100]

Chapter 10 and 11 in Romans involve the subject of *faith* in relation to Israel's current rejection (chap. 10) and Israel's future restoration (chap. 11), which the reader is prepared for by these last few verses here in Romans 9. But here (chap. 9), Paul provides us the *reason* for Israel's temporary blindness —their unbelief—which is manifested in a system of **works righteousness**.

> Israel as a whole, excluding the believing remnant, failed to gain a righteous standing before God because she tried to win it with works. A stone on the racetrack over which she stumbled impeded her progress. Intent on winning in her own effort Israel failed to recognize the Stone prophesied in Scripture who was to provide salvation for her. ...

God intended the Messiah to be the provider of salvation. However the Jews did not allow Him to fulfill this function for them. Consequently this Stone became a stumbling block for them (cf. 1Cor. 1:23).[101]

Attempting to develop a relationship with God through a system of good works or rule keeping is part of the human condition. From the Garden of Eden (Gen. 3) to the present, man has sought to hide his nakedness and shame before God through an elaborate system of good works and religious performance. It is natural (for our sin nature anyway) to try to offset the bad we do by counterbalancing with some good. Inherently, we know that there is something wrong so we try by human wisdom to solve the problem. Curiously, we tend to do this independent from the God we desire to satisfy. In other words, we do not ask Him what He wants us to do, but set off on a pathway of our own to please God. This is typically because of the guilt which sin imposes on our conscience and the deceptive effects it has on our thinking (cf. Heb. 3:13). In the Garden of Eden, Adam and Eve tried to hide their nakedness with fig leaves which is an apropos picture of human effort attempting to mask the shame of sin's guilt. Replacing the fig leaves with some system of human concoction of good works and elaborate ritual has been the tragic history of man ever since the fall. We see it manifested in the various religions of the world after its introduction of an elaborate system of idolatry and rituals at the Tower of Babel (cf. Gen. 11), as they attempted to build a stairway to the heaven they believed awaited them. Today this has translated into many world religions creating their own stairway to heaven, though their roots are traceable back to the Tower of Babel. Man innately knows that he must reach something beyond this life, and he works hard to figure out a way to get there. However, since man cannot remedy the problem on his own, God promised a Deliverer.

God's promise to solve the sin problem (Gen. 3:15) is traceable through the early chapters of Genesis to the call of Abraham in chapter 12. God chose to call this man from among pagan idolaters (cf. Joshua 24:2) to create a nation, bring the Deliverer to this world, and remedy all the damage caused by sin. Additionally, this newly created nation through Abraham, Isaac, and Jacob had the responsibility of safekeeping God's revelation. But from the very beginning, it was understood that God only received man because of his *faith*, not his good works. Thus, when Moses (a type of the Deliverer to come, cf. Acts 7:35) arrived on the scene hundreds of years after Abraham's experience of justification (Gen. 15:6), the Law given through him to Israel did not change or replace the principle of salvation by *faith* (Gal. 3:17, 18). For God made promises to Abraham of land, descendants, and redemptive blessing to the world that He ratified into an unconditional covenant (Gen. 15). If there was ever a nation that should have understood that works could not provide salvation, Israel should have well known. Indeed, it is the reason for their creation—ontologically—why they exist in the first place.

How did so many of those in Israel conclude that they could be acceptable to God by good works? Certainly, as in Paul's OT quotes used to support his points, Israel was not morally superior to the pagan nations that were destroyed by the severity of God's judgment. Paul himself at one time trapped in that same self-righteousness as his kinsmen, expressed the reason for the blindness. In 2 Cor. 3:9-16 he said contrasting the old and new covenants:

> For if the ministry of condemnation has glory, then the ministry of justification has an overwhelming glory. In fact, that which once had glory lost its glory, because the other glory surpassed it. For if that which fades away came through glory, how much more does that which is permanent have glory? Therefore, since we have such a hope, we speak very boldly, not like Moses, who kept covering his face with a veil to keep the people of Israel from gazing at the end of what was fading away. However, their minds were hardened, for to this day the same veil is still there when they read the old covenant. Only in union

with the Messiah is that veil removed. Yet even to this day, when Moses is read, a veil covers their hearts. But whenever a person turns to the Lord, the veil is removed. (ISV)

The solution to a works based self-righteousness before God is faith in Christ. Yet, it is the simplicity of *faith* in Christ that is the *stumbling block* for Jews––the very argument Paul gives in the passage under consideration.

How did so many Israelites arrive at these legalistic conclusions? Did they forget or ignore their history? The seven feasts of Leviticus were established to help them abide in the remembrance of what God did for the nation in delivering them from both Egypt and pagan sinfulness. The five sacrifices in the first seven chapters of Leviticus were given to allow the priests to approach an otherwise unapproachable Holy God and atone for both the sins of the people and their own sin natures. Both sacrifices and feasts were the means of sanctifying the nation of Israel in their relationship with God. However, at some point the sin issues the law was designed to address were traded for the law itself. Instead of appreciating the fact that God elected to create the nation and eventually gave them the law to educate and manage their relationship with Him, they saw themselves as the end reason for the law. In other words, they saw something intrinsic in themselves nationally that was missing in other nations—they thought they had intrinsic moral excellence. Instead of viewing the law as a training vehicle that enabled God to work through them to reach the world, they viewed it as an end reward for their righteousness. In a gross miscalculation, they exchanged the mercy of God that they initially appreciated for a self-exalted attitude of entitlement of covenant privileges. In short, they thought God gave them the law because they were better, that He created a better nation of people through Abraham. This is the genealogical or race benefit fallacy where bloodlines are supposed to pass on intellectual, moral, and spiritual benefits to the offspring. In an ironically tragic twist, it was this way of thinking that motivated Hitler's systematic murder of the Jews to weed out their inferior genetics. However, genetics does not carry our moral or spiritual capabilities. If this was the case, Abraham's first son Ishmael would have been intrinsically better than other people. Yet, Ishmael received no covenant privileges or Messianic promises for his offspring. This is because tracing bloodlines is not the issue. God's purpose in election—including the nation of Israel—is to establish the path of the Messianic genealogy so when He arrived everyone would know He was the Deliverer from God. One look at the genealogy of Jesus Christ will tell you there is nothing special genetically in that list—it may even be to the contrary. So why would Israel think that the physical birth of anyone in Isaac's lineage would have more intrinsic worth than Ishmael would? Both lineages work their way back to the same father, Abraham. Moreover, how could they conclude that keeping certain laws would make them righteous before God? As Paul said earlier in Romans, "For if Abraham were justified by works, he hath whereof to glory; but not before God" (4:2). Therefore, the connection of being God's special people (Exodus 19:5; Deut. 14:2) with a thought of intrinsic worth that is above other nations provided a twisted foundation for works righteousness.

Israel is special because they were in a covenant relationship with God. He gave them the law because they needed it for national and individual spiritual development in the truth. They needed to obey the law to receive the blessings, benefits, privileges available to them in their relationship with God. But they twisted the purpose of the law along the way to their own hurt. This change does not happen overnight. It took a few hundred years after their return from the Babylonian captivity—which they suffered because of their idolatry and deplorable sin—to develop this attitude of self-righteousness. Unfortunately, when God bestows benefits—not due to a person's righteousness but His grace alone—they can be misunderstood as if intrinsically deserved instead of the blessings of His grace. When the whole panorama of Bible history is taken into view, no one should conclude that man has any intrinsic righteousness acceptable to God, and it is for that reason He promised to send a Deliverer because man is lost in sin. Israel should have been thoroughly educated on this subject since God vouchsafed His revelation to them. They only had to read the word God secured to their keeping because the answers were readily available in black and white.

33 As it is written, Behold, I lay in Sion a stumblingstone and rock of offence: and whosoever believeth on him shall not be ashamed.

This final verse refers back to both Isaiah 8:14 and 28:16. Isaiah prophetically announced that God would bring His Messiah (*him*) to Zion which would cause both *stumbling* and *offense*. As MacDonald comments, "This is exactly what the Lord foretold through Isaiah. The Messiah's coming to Jerusalem would have a twofold effect. To some people He would prove to be a stumbling stone and rock of offense (Isa. 8:14). Others would believe on Him and find no reason for shame, offense, or disappointment (Isa. 28:16)."[102] Thus, two opposite responses to *him* should have been anticipated when He arrived: rejection and acceptance. We also learn the psalmist anticipated His arrival. In Psalm 118:22 it says, "The stone which the builders refused is become the head stone of the corner." The *stone* would not only cause *stumbling*, but would be the very cornerstone for establishing the building of God's people. The cornerstone is the foundation-stone upon which the structure rested in the building of the temple, from which every other stone in the temple's construction is built—He is the cornerstone of God's redemptive work upon which His people are built. Peter referred to this building of God's people when he said, "you also, as living stones, are being built up a spiritual house, a holy priesthood, to offer up spiritual sacrifices acceptable to God through Jesus Christ" (1 Peter 2:5, NKJV). Moreover, Jesus applied this *cornerstone* reference to Himself so there would be no mistake He was the anticipated Messiah. But why should the anticipated Messiah cause people to *stumble* over Him? Because the Messiah is anticipated in the Law of Moses, the prophets, and many types in the OT. He was expected to be a reigning king and inaugurate a government that would fulfill all the promises and prophecies for Israel. The idea that a man from humble means in the poor town of Nazareth and an unremarkably ordinary family could be the Messiah was too much for the Jewish leadership to accept.

When at the temple in Jerusalem near the end of His ministry, Jesus spoke a parable against the chief priests, scribes and elders and made the application to Himself by quoting Psalm 118:22-23: "Haven't you read this Scripture: The stone that the builders rejected—this has become the cornerstone. This came from the Lord and is wonderful in our eyes" (Mark 12:10, 11, HCSB)? His application was not lost on them: "Now they wanted to arrest him (but they feared the crowd), because they realized that he told this parable against them. So they left him and went away" (Mark 12:12, NET). After all the work and elaborate system of rules the Jewish leadership had constructed over the years, the concept that God would accept people by simple faith in the Messiah required a humility unable to scale the high walls of pride they had built.

God's interest has always been people. He created man and His love for man is a theme that not only permeates Scripture, but also answers why He endures with such longsuffering to reach man. Indeed, the sacrifice of His Son should speak volumes of the great measure of God's gracious love He has for all people. Any attempt to limit the scope of His love to man who He created in His image flies in the face of God's nature, character, and acts. Calvinism is a cold system of legal emphasis on God's anger against sinners and emphasizes that man is nothing but miserable, entirely depraved, and an offense to God by his mere existence. Though some of the views in Calvinism regarding God's judicial perspective of man are correct, their essential perspective is lopsided and off point. Calvinists strike from the perspective that one would wonder why God would save anyone because they are such miserable sinners. Though it is true that man is a miserable sinner and in need of redemption from his path of eternal ruin, the Scripture emphasizes God's love and mercy toward those He made in His image. The condemnation of man is a scriptural fact which is clearly stated throughout the Bible. That is why God sent His Son in mercy to redeem man. Indeed, Micah instructed the nation of Israel what God required from them, "to do justly, and to love mercy, and to walk humbly with thy God" (Micah 6:8). Why? Because God loves mercy and wanted Israel to be merciful just as God is merciful. This explains why Jesus reprimands the Pharisees when He said, "But go ye and learn what that meaneth, I will have mercy, and not sacrifice: for I am not come to call the righteous, but sinners to repentance" (Matt. 9:13), for He desired mercy above sacrifice. Downplaying the tremendous mercy God extends to miserable sinners is a mistake. There is the judicial aspect of man's redemption in justification that deserves the utmost respect theologically, for it explains how God puts man "in Christ." However, it does not explain why He did it. He did it because of His great love and desire to restore man to his original position of fellowship, and by doing it bring all the glory to God. However, I believe Calvinists tend to underemphasize the *why*, because they are obsessed with the *how*—which they believe is deterministic, and ultimately ends in a fatalistic view of God's acts.

Paul describes the legality of man's separation from God in his epistles so that the instructive elements of what Jesus did for sinners can be understood and appreciated. The grace and mercy shown is set in contrast to the condemnation, so the redemptive work can be developed and properly understood. Yet this is not the emphasis of the epistles entirely, but establishes the foundation for the motivation and encouragement to walk with God and properly represent Him. The epistles— Paul's in particular—emphasize God's great love, mercy, and grace shown in the plan of redemption as the basis for the follow-on application to walk with Jesus. Understanding man's condemnation is foundational to the entire plan of God's remarkable redemption through His Son. Knowing the *how* of redemption helps us appreciate the *why* of redemption; they must work together. The overall theme of the Bible is God's long-suffering in the redemptive program to rescue man from his eternal ruin. The entire story combines the balance of both how He did it and why He did it. Therefore, to overemphasize one against the other in variance to the balance of Scripture is a mistake. Both are necessary for understanding and appreciation.

A person must know they are drowning before they will receive help. Indeed, only after a person is saved from drowning will they appreciate the rescuer's efforts. Jesus made this point clear that He was the Rescuer when He said, "They that be whole need not a physician, but they that are sick. But go ye and learn what that meaneth, I will have mercy, and not sacrifice: for I am not come to call the righteous, but sinners to repentance" (Matt. 9:12-13). Only sick people want a doctor and only sinners need a Savior, but they need to recognize their need before they want help. The gospel (good news) is only a gospel to those who recognize their need to be saved. Again, Jesus inextricably connects mercy to the context of His redemptive work when He says He wants the Jews to know that God wants mercy before sacrifice. If we leave mercy behind in our quest to understand God's redemptive plan, we remove a main feature. If we limit His mercy to certain people from eternity past, we remove Scripture. For Paul says, "God hath concluded them all in unbelief, that he might have mercy upon all" (Rom. 11:32). Ironically, Paul refers to the Jews in this verse, the very ones that he initially pleaded for when he entered his instruction regarding Israel at the beginning of Romans 9. These Jews are the ones Calvinists would eliminate from God's mercy because of their national rejection of Christ. However, Paul says that God includes them all in the category of those to whom mercy is available to. Why? Because the qualification is their unbelief (Rom. 11:32), the very element most Calvinists would determine removes them from God's mercy.

Finally, Paul makes a key point in his quote when he says,

whosoever believeth on him shall not be ashamed. The offer is to *whosoever* and as has been shown, if God makes an offer, it has to be genuine and not disingenuous, for this would impinge upon His character. Those who do *believe on Him shall not be ashamed* because of the very fact that they can trust His word— His offer. If the offer were disingenuous, perhaps they would be *ashamed*. The promise of Scripture is that trust in God will never leave a person disgraced or dishonored (lit. put to shame). This offer to *whosoever* creates a problem for many Calvinists, some vehemently disagree with gospel preaching through crusades. In their minds, offering Christ to the masses (*whosoever*) could result in creating a situation where the gospel is offered to those who are non-elect, thus deceiving them into thinking they can be saved when they cannot be. Some believe—as Calvin was quoted under the chapter on Perseverance of the Saints —that some people will believe, but not actually be redeemed because they are not elect, but would result in being *ashamed*. This is a monumental problem Calvinists face if they follow the faulty views of their leader. These Calvinists seem to grasp that a disingenuous offer of the gospel is possible if they do not control the means of its dissemination (i.e. to crowds). However, they seem to miss the point that Jesus, Peter, and Paul did not abide by their concerns and did offer to crowds. This ought to instruct them that there is a problem with their theology, but unfortunately they run their perspectives through Calvin before they run it through the Bible—a tragic error.

No matter what any Calvinist declares or pontificates, the Scriptures state that the gospel is available to *whosoever* and *believing* it results in never being *ashamed*. The fact that we are all sinners means we are entirely at the mercy of God. However, knowing the nature and character of God, "It is better to trust in the LORD than to put confidence in man" (Psalm 118:8). There is no risk to trust the Lord and believe in Jesus Christ. He declared so, therefore in doing so, we will never be *ashamed*.

CONCLUSION

If you made it this far in the book, I hope you rediscovered Romans 9. If you were of a Calvinistic persuasion, I appreciate the fact that you made it this far and hope the preparatory chapters and exposition enlightened you to a straight forward non-Calvinistic view. Moreover, I hope you see God's nature and character in the light of Scripture and appreciate Him even more. I did not have to work hard to make the case that all people are savable; the Scripture does that and I only pointed out the verses. However, if you maintain your Calvinistic perspectives, that is your own choice, I hope you realize that conundrum—it is up to you.

If you did not have a Calvinistic persuasion when you started this book, I hope your view of God has grown along with an appreciation of the redemptive plan He devised and accomplished on your behalf. It doesn't matter who you are; Jesus Christ went to the cross for you. The plan God put into place from eternity was founded upon His love and mercy, brought into operation by His grace and power. Our redemption is by His grace and not our works or effort, but He does require we receive it by faith—our own faith. Not a coerced or forced faith, but faith freely exercised in response to His marvelous grace and love.

There is no need to rehash all the arguments developed in this book, but I do want to leave you with a thought if at this point you are not convinced that Calvin's theological positions are biblically skewed. We must ask why Satan would attempt to blind anyone if man is already blinded from birth—one of the non-elect, who will never see, hear, or respond to the gospel or any truth at all. Paul says "if our gospel be hid, it is hid to them that are lost: In whom the god of this world hath blinded the minds of them which believe not, lest the light of the glorious gospel of Christ" (2 Cor. 4:3-4). Paul says Satan has blinded those who are lost; he does not accuse God of doing that. Paul also uses the word "hid", meaning to conceal or cover. Satan takes advantage of their unbelief—"them which believe not"—and causes their blindness to conceal the truth of the gospel. Of the word "blinded", Robertson says, "**Blinded** (*etuphlōsen*). First aorist active of *tuphloō*, old verb to blind (*tuphlos*, blind). They refused to believe (*apistōn*) and so Satan got the power to blind their thoughts. That happens with willful disbelievers."[103] Satan obviously knows something of which Calvinists refuse to acknowledge. Again, the claim of Paul does not make sense in the context of Calvinistic determinism. If a person is not savable, why make sure they stay that way? If the argument is that Satan does not know if a person is elect and therefore tries to blind everyone in hopes of blinding the elect, that view fails its own principle. If the elect will be converted because of determinism, Paul would know this, and actively blinding a person is a useless exercise since God will make them believe by irresistible grace. In other words, any attempt to blind is a fruitless effort in light of determinism. We know this from the grammar explained by Robertson and Paul's context regarding those who refuse to accept his gospel. Satan is a liar and deceiver, but his attempts to lie to the elect and deceive them into blindness is a silly way to represent him in Scripture if it is not possible to do it. And then blame him for their blindness—why credit him with something he is unable to accomplish? As already mentioned, Paul also said Satan hindered him (1 Thess. 2:18), which means that Satan could also do that. In a deterministic framework, it would be God who makes Satan blind people and hinder Paul. This is a nonsensical view of sacred Scripture and beneath the dignity and inspiration of the Holy Spirit and integrity of the authors, not to mention a very confusing theology of the acts of God.

Also mentioned earlier, to disprove Calvinistic determinism, only some clear references from the Bible would be necessary, not the examination of every single verse in question. The actual burden of proof is on the Calvinist to make their case from an examination of the whole Bible to prove there is no libertarian free will, but this has yet to be done because it cannot be done. The Scriptures are replete with examples of stories, statements, instructions, and pleas that are unintelligible apart from the libertarian free will context. Are there times that God determines the outcome of events? Of course! But it does not logically follow that God determines all events. Since free will events represent the normal reading of the text, the burden is to those who claim otherwise (by their own free will).

Finally, my hope is that there is a recognition that without the existence of libertarian free will, God's power and glory when interacting with man is actually diminished rather than magnified. In the minds of Calvinists, God has no way to control what He does not determine. However, if even fallible human beings can have control over events that they do not determine, then how much more can the omnipotent, sovereign God of all creation? The Son of God can determine to take on a sinless human nature being born from a sinful human mother. The Holy Spirit can determine to bring inerrant Scriptures from fallible human authors. These determinative activities are accomplished without altering the sinful natures or free will of the individuals and bring about perfect outcomes of both those events. If that is so, why cannot God allow libertarian free will in the salvation process, prophecy, or any other event and still bring about the outcome He desires? He's God! To claim God cannot is to severely limit Him to the conceptions of the minds of men and commit the actual error they attempt to avoid—diminishing His sovereignty! God was abundantly clear when He said through the prophet, "For my thoughts are not your thoughts, neither are your ways my ways, saith the LORD. For as the heavens are higher than the earth, so are my ways higher than your ways, and my thoughts than your thoughts" (Isaiah 55:8-9). Since we cannot think on God's level or fully comprehend what He does, we are instructed to obey

202

His word that reveals what He wants us to know and are capable of apprehending. Having said that, the verses previous to those just quoted say, "Seek ye the LORD while he may be found, call ye upon him while he is near: Let the wicked forsake his way, and the unrighteous man his thoughts: and let him return unto the LORD, and he will have mercy upon him; and to our God, for he will abundantly pardon" (Isaiah 55:6-7). In other words, God appeals to man who He made in His image to turn from their sin and seek Him. How can these verses be explained apart from libertarian free will? Moreover, if you do concoct a deterministic interpretation that satisfies you, did you arrive at that decision by your own free will? If not, how would you make that determination?

---

[1] Hermeneutics is the principle used to interpret the Bible. Since the Bible is a historical document, written in a grammatical construct and assumed to be literal (normal) in its communication, the hermeneutical method followed in this book is the literal, historical, grammatical method.

[2] Martin, Walter. "Appendix B: Faith Movement." *The Kingdom of the Cults*, Bethany House Publishers, 1997.

[3] Martin, Walter. "Chapter 7: Christian Science." *The Kingdom of the Cults*, Bethany House Publishers, 1997.

[4] Theological Determinism is the belief that God causes all events to occur, that they are foreordained or predestined to happen. This includes good and evil. Philosophically, it is a form of fatalism meaning that no matter what people do, they cannot change any aspect of the course of events since they are fixed.

[5] Sire, James. *Why Should Anyone Believe Anything At All.* Kindle Ed., InterVarsity Press. 2010.

[6] Pascal, Blaise. *The Thoughts of Blaise Pascal.* Thomas Whittaker Bible House, 1888, p 206-7.

[7] Harris, Ralph W., M.A. "Galatians-Philemon." *Complete Biblical Library Commentary,* executive editor, Stanley M. Horton, Th.D. Dagengruppen AB. Database, 1995, WORDsearch Corp. World Library Press, Inc., 2009.

[8] Robertson, A.T. *Word Pictures in the New Testament*, Vol. IV, Baker Book House, 1931, p.525.

[9] Vincent, Marvin R. *Word Studies in the New Testament*, 2nd ed., Vol. III, MacDonald Publishing, 1975, p. 376.

[10] Alford, Henry. *The New Testament for English Readers*, Moody Press. p. 1216.

[11] Nicoll, W.R. *The Expositor's Greek Testament*, Vol. III, Wm. B. Eerdmans Publishing Company, 1983, p. 19.

[12] Vine, W.E. *Vine's Expository Dictionary of New Testament Words.* Fleming H. Revell, 1981, p. 146.

[13] Wuest, Kenneth. *Word Studies in the Greek New Testament*, vol. 1, Wm. B. Eerdmans Publishing Company, 1995, p. 69.

[14] Calvin, John. *Commentary on Galatians and Ephesians. Christian Classics Ethereal Library,* https://ccel.org/ccel/calvin/calcom41/calcom41/Page_228.html .

[15] Geisler, Norman L. and Thomas Howe. *When Critics Ask: A Popular Handbook on Bible Difficulties*, Victor Books, 1992, p. 475-6.

[16] Guzik, David. "Ephesians Chapter 2." *Enduring Word*, 25 Apr. 2019, enduringword.com/bible-commentary/ephesians-2/.

[17] Dawkins, Richard. *The Blind Watchmaker.* W. W. Norton &Company Inc., New York, 1986, p.1.

[18] Crick, Francis. *What Mad Pursuit.* Basic Books Inc., New York, 1988, p.138.

[19] Warfield, B.B. "Compatibilism." *Monergism*, 2018, https://www.monergism.com/topics/free-will/compatibilism .

[20] Talbot, Mark. "All the Good That Is Ours in Christ: Seeing God's Gracious Hand in the Hurts Others Do to Us." *Desiring God*, Oct. 2005, www.desiringgod.org/messages/all-the-good-that-is-ours-in-christ-seeing-gods-gracious-hand-in-the-hurts-others-do-to-us , Accessed 12 January 2020.

[21] "Does God Cause Evil? A Calvinist Response by James White." *YouTube*,

uploaded by Bible Answer Man, 10 Aug. 2018, https://www.youtube.com/watch?v=B4b3B9gR_78.

[22] Rogers, Ronnie W. *Reflections of a Disenchanted Calvinist: The Disquieting Realities of Calvinism*, Kindle Ed., WestBow Press, 2016.

[23] Warfield, B.B. "Compatibilism." *Monergism*, 2018, https://www.monergism.com/topics/free-will/compatibilism .

[24] Rogers, Ronnie W. *Reflections of a Disenchanted Calvinist: The Disquieting Realities of Calvinism*, Kindle Ed., WestBow Press, 2016.

[25] *Reprobate* is an adjective (adokimos) Paul uses in Romans 1:28 to describe a rejected, depraved or worthless mind. The main idea is rejection; therefore in Calvinism, the reprobate are those not elected to salvation, but "elected" to damnation prior to their existence by God.

[26] *Free will* from a non-Calvinistic perspective is the belief that man's will is actually free, which is termed "Libertarian free will." In this view, free will is logically incompatible with a deterministic universe.

[27] For an excellent analysis, see Edgar, Thomas R. "The Meaning Of ΠΡΟΓΙΝΩΣΚΩ ('To Foreknow')." *Chafer Theological Seminary Journal*, vol. 9, no. 1, Galaxie Software Electronic Publishing, Spring, 2003, https://www.galaxie.com/article/ctsj09-1-03.

[28] Toplady, Augustus, "Rock of Ages." 1763, *The Gospel Magazine*, 1775.

[29] Telford, Andrew. *Subjects of Sovereignty: Adoption, Predestination, Election, Foreknowledge.* WORDsearch Corp., 1980, p. 43.

[30] Vincent, Marvin R. *Word Studies in the New Testament.* 2nd ed., vol. 3, MacDonald Publishing, 1975, p. 48.

[31] Rogers, Ronnie W. *Reflections of a Disenchanted Calvinist: The Disquieting Realities of Calvinism.* Kindle Ed. ed., West Bow Press, 2016, locations 2353-2355.

[32] Rogers, Ronnie W. *Reflections of a Disenchanted Calvinist: The Disquieting Realities of Calvinism.* Kindle Ed. ed., West Bow Press, 2016, locations 2353-2355.

[33] This article is a prime example of text torturing. Tweeddale, John. "What Does 'World' Mean in John 3:16?" *Ligonier Ministries*, 31 July 2020, www.ligonier.org/blog/what-does-world-mean-john-316/.

[34] For fuller treatments on this subject of Limited Atonement see: Allen, David L. *The Extent of the Atonement, A Historical and Critical Review.* B&H Academic, 1 November 2016. and Rogers, Ronnie W. *Does God Love All or Some?: Comparing Biblical Extensivism and Cavinism's Exclusivism.* Wipf & Stock, 14 May 2019.

[35] Meyer, Heinrich August Wilhelm. "2 Cor. 5:19." *Critical and Exegetical Commentary on the New Testament*, E-Sword ed., T. & T. Clark, Edinburgh,

1879.

[36] Shank, Robert. *Elect in the Son.* Kindle ed., Baker Publishing Group, 1989, locations 2435-2436.

[37] Tozer, A.W. *Knowledge of the Holy.* Electronic ed., Harper & Row, 1961, p. 76.

[38] See the article: Cannon, Stephen F. *THE BOSTON CHURCH OF CHRIST Has Mind Control Come to Beantown?* 1989, http://www.reveal.org/library/psych/beantown.html.

[39] Calvin, John. *A Treatise of the Eternal Predestination of God.* Kindle ed., Fig, 2013, location 201-204. Full quote from this reference appears in the next chapter.

[40] Anderson, David R. "The Soteriological Impact Of Augustine's Change From Premillennialism To Amillennialism Part Two." https://faithalone.org/wp-content/uploads/2020/06/anderson.pdf

[41] Calvin, John. *Institutes of the Christian Religion.* book 3, ch. 2, sec. 11, The Westminster Press, 1960, p. 555.

[42] Wilson, Ken. *The Foundation of Augustinian-Calvinism.* Regula Fidei Press, 2019.

[43] Lucius Annaeus Seneca Quotes. (n.d.). *Quotes.net.* STANDS4 LLC, 2019. Web. 12 Dec. 2019. https://www.quotes.net/quote/8616.

[44] "Manichaeism." *Manichaeism - New World Encyclopedia.* https://www.newworldencyclopedia.org/entry/Manichaeism. Accessed 12 Dec. 2019.

[45] "Augustine of Hippo." *Augustine of Hippo - New World Encyclopedia,* www.newworldencyclopedia.org/entry/Augustine_of_Hippo. Accessed 12 Dec. 2019.

[46] Calvin, John. *A Treatise of the Eternal Predestination of God.* Kindle ed., Fig, 2013. Locations 201-4.

[47] Calvin, John. *Institutes of the Christian Religion.* book 3, ch. 21, sec. 5, The Westminster Press, 1960, p. 926.

[48] Calvin, John. *Institutes of the Christian Religion.* book 3, chap 21, sec 7, The Westminster Press, 1960, p. 931.

[49] Calvin, John. *Institutes of the Christian Religion.* book 3, chap 22, sec 11, The Westminster Press, 1960, p. 947.

[50] Calvin, John. *Commentary on Catholic Epistles. Christian Classics Ethereal Library,* https://ccel.org/ccel/calvin/calcom45/calcom45.vii.iv.iii.html .

[51] Blunt, J.J. B.D. *"Undesigned Coincidences In The Writings Of The Old and New Testament, An Argument Of Their Veracity"* Robert Carter & Brothers, New York, 1851.

[52] Shank, Robert. *Elect in the Son*. Kindle ed., Bethany House Publishers, 1989, Location 635.

[53] Modalism is a heresy that understands God as a Being not having the three Persons of the Trinity, but sees the Father, Son and Holy Spirit as the same "Person" appearing in different "modes."

[54] Tertullian. "Against Praxeas." *Anti-Nicene Fathers*, Vol 3. sect. VII. Ch. 11

[55] Morgan, G. Campbell. "Christian Citizenship: No Abiding City." *The Westminster Pulpit*, Baker Book House, 1985, p. 141.

[56] Epistemology is the study of knowledge, or how we know what we know.

[57] Ontology is the study of the nature of being, or why something exists.

[58] Materialism is the belief that physical matter is the ultimate reality and all that exists. This means that man's mind and consciousness are the by-products of the material process, i.e. nothing transcends the material world.

[59] Thayer, Joseph Henry. *Greek-English Lexicon Of The New Testament*. Harper & Brothers, American Book Company, 1889, p. 453.

[60] Vincent, Marvin R. *Word Studies in the New Testament*, 2nd ed., Vol. III, MacDonald Publishing, 1975, p. 4.

[61] Robertson, A.T. *Word Pictures in the New Testament*. vol. IV, Baker Book House, 1931, p. 324

[62] Robertson , A.T. Romans 9:8" *Robertson's Word Pictures of the New Testament*, *Biblestudytools.com*, https://www.biblestudytools.com/commentaries/robertsons-word-pictures/romans/romans-9-8.html. Accessed 18 Mar. 2020.

[63] Robertson, A.T. "Romans 9:9." *Robertson's Word Pictures of the New Testament*, *Biblestudytools.com*, https://www.biblestudytools.com/commentaries/robertsons-word-pictures/romans/romans-9-9.html. Accessed 18 Mar. 2020.

[64] MacDonald, William. "Romans 9:9."*Believer's Bible Commentary*, E-Sword ed., Thomas Nelson, 2008.

[65] Vincent, Marvin R. *Word Studies in the New Testament*. 2nd ed., Vol. III, MacDonald Publishing, 1975, p. 102.

[66] Coke, Thomas. *A Commentary on the Holy Bible*. vol. 2, London, 1803, p. 102.

[67] Telford, Andrew. *Subjects of Sovereignty: Adoption, Predestination, Election, Foreknowledge*. WORDsearch Corp, 1980, p. 46, 57.

[68] Telford, Andrew. *Subjects of Sovereignty: Adoption, Predestination, Election, Foreknowledge*. WORDsearch Corp, 1980, p. 56-57.

[69] Telford, Andrew. *Subjects of Sovereignty: Adoption, Predestination, Election, Foreknowledge*. WORDsearch Corp, 1980, p. 56.

[70] Whedon, Daniel D. "Acts - Romans." *A Popular Commentary of the New Testament*, vol. 3, Hodder and Stoughton, London, 1875, p. 358.

[71] Whedon, Daniel D. "Acts - Romans." *A Popular Commentary of the New Testament*, vol. 3, Hodder and Stoughton, London, 1875, p. 358.

[72] MacDonald, William. "Romans 9:15 note." *Believer's Bible Commentary*, E-Sword ed., Thomas Nelson, 2008.

[73] Vincent, Marvin R. *Word Studies in the New Testament*, 2nd ed., Vol. III, MacDonald Publishing, 1975, p. 104.

[74] Coke, Thomas. *A Commentary on the Holy Bible.* vol. 2, London, 1803, p. 104.

[75] Hindson, Dr. Ed. *King James Version Bible Commentary*. Thomas Nelson Publishers, Inc., 1999, p. 86.

[76] Godet, Fredric Louis. *St. Paul's Epistle to the Romans.* Funk & Wagnalls, New York, 1883, p. 354.

[77] MacDonald, William. "Romans 9:18 note." *Believer's Bible Commentary*, E-Sword ed., Thomas Nelson, 2008.

[78] Constable, Thomas. "Isaiah 29:15." *Expository Notes of Dr. Constable*, E-Sword ed., Tyndale Seminary Press, 2012. 12 vols.

[79] Constable, Thomas. "Isaiah 29:16." *Expository Notes of Dr. Constable*, E-Sword ed., Tyndale Seminary Press, 2012. 12 vols.

[80] Constable, Thomas. "Romans 9:21." *Expository Notes of Dr. Constable*, E-Sword ed., Tyndale Seminary Press, 2012. 12 vols.

[81] Whedon, Daniel D. "Acts - Romans." *A Popular Commentary of the New Testament*, vol. 3, Hodder and Stoughton, London, 1875, p. 362.

[82] Vincent, Marvin R. *Word Studies in the New Testament*, 2nd ed., Vol. III, MacDonald Publishing, 1975, p. 107 .

[83] Godet, Fredric Louis. *St. Paul's Epistle to the Romans.* Funk & Wagnalls, New York, 1883, p. 363.

[84] Godet, Fredric Louis. *St. Paul's Epistle to the Romans.* Funk & Wagnalls, New York, 1883, p. 363-4.

[85] Barnes, Albert. *Notes Explanatory and Practical on the Epistle to the Romans.* 9th ed., Harpers and Brothers, New York, 1863, p. 203.

[86] Coke, Thomas. *A Commentary on the Holy Bible.* vol. 2, London, 1803, p.55.

[87] MacDonald, William. "Romans 9:25 note." *Believer's Bible Commentary*, E-Sword ed., Thomas Nelson, 2008.

[88] Whedon, Daniel D. "Acts - Romans." *A Popular Commentary of the New Testament*, vol. 3, Hodder and Stoughton, London, 1875, p. 363.

[89] MacDonald, William. "Ephesians 2:12 note." *Believer's Bible*

Commentary, E-Sword ed., Thomas Nelson, 2008.

[90] MacDonald, William. "Ephesians 3:6 note." *Believer's Bible Commentary*, E-Sword ed., Thomas Nelson, 2008.

[91] Barnes, Albert. *Notes Explanatory and Practical on the Epistle to the Romans*, 9th ed., Harpers and Brothers, New York, 1863, p. 205.

[92] Whedon, Daniel D. "Acts - Romans." *A Popular Commentary of the New Testament*, vol. 3, Hodder and Stoughton, London, 1875, p. 363.

[93] Constable, Thomas. "Isaiah 10:23." *Expository Notes of Dr. Constable*, E-Sword ed., Tyndale Seminary Press, 2012, 12 vols.

[94] Constable, Thomas. "Romans 9:28." *Expository Notes of Dr. Constable*, E-Sword ed., Tyndale Seminary Press, 2012, 12 vols.

[95] Coke, Thomas. ""Reflections under Romans 9." *A Commentary on the Holy Bible*, E-sword ed.

[96] Whedon, Daniel D. "Acts - Romans." *A Popular Commentary of the New Testament*, vol. 3, Hodder and Stoughton, London, 1875, p. 364.

[97] Whedon, Daniel D. "Acts - Romans." *A Popular Commentary of the New Testament*, vol. 3, Hodder and Stoughton, London, 1875, p. 363.

[98] Coke, Thomas. *A Commentary on the Holy Bible. vol. 2*, London, 1803, p. 107.

[99] Whedon, Daniel D. "Acts - Romans." *A Popular Commentary of the New Testament,* vol.3, Hodder and Stoughton, London, 1875, p. 364.

[100] Godet, Fredric Louis. *St. Paul's Epistle to the Romans*, Funk & Wagnalls, New York, 1883, p. 369.

[101] Constable, Thomas. "Romans 9:32-33." *Expository Notes of Dr. Constable*, E-Sword ed., Tyndale Seminary Press, 2012, 12 vols.

[102] MacDonald, William. "Romans 9:33 note." *Believer's Bible Commentary*, E-Sword ed. Thomas Nelson, 2008.

[103] Robertson, A.T. *Word Pictures in the New Testament, vol. IV*, Baker Book House, 1931, p. 224-5.

ACKNOWLEDGEMENT

I could not have completed this book without the help of others. I would like to thank Kate Hanley for her skillful editing and creativity, Herb Butterworth for his honest assessment of the initial manuscript, and the encouragement of other friends along with way.

Most importantly I would like to thank my wife, her example of faith and continued encouragement is a constant support of my work and service to the Lord in all areas. She is a true inspiration.

ABOUT THE AUTHOR

Scott Mitchell

Scott Mitchell is the assistant pastor of Calvary Chapel of Boston since it began in 1989. He has written multiple pamphlets on various Bible subjects. He teaches high school Bible, apologetics and ethics classes at Calvary Chapel Academy, and a weekly discipleship class focused on various Bible topics and Christian apologetics. He has been married since 1983.

BOOKS BY THIS AUTHOR

God Of Covenants: God's Unchanging Nature In Changing Covenants

How do we know who God is and what He wants from us? Many things are said about God, but what does God say about Himself? Does the Bible give us these answers? How should we approach the Bible in the first place? Why does God have different rules and consequences in the Old Testament than He does in the New Testament? What are the conditions for having a relationship with God throughout human history? Do they change? What are the conditions today? These and many more questions are answered in this book.

God of Covenants covers a wide range of issues related to God, the Bible, and His people. The various covenants in the Bible are put into historical and covenantal perspective for the reader. The chronology of the Bible is seen through the lens of what the Bible itself teaches. This book will connect dots for both the experienced and the beginning reader of Scripture that are crucial to comprehending the Bible in the context it is written. This book reduces years of study into a simple to understand presentation, laying the foundation for more rewarding personal Bible study.

Made in the USA
Monee, IL
03 October 2024

67099156R00125